TUCKALEECHEE COVE

TUCKALEECHEE COVE

A Passage through Time

Boyce N. Driskell and Robert J. Norrell

The University of Tennessee Press
Knoxville

First Edition.

Photographs and drawings not otherwise credited are by the staff of the Townsend Archaeological Project and the Archaeological Research Laboratory, University of Tennessee, Knoxville.

The paper in this book meets the requirements of American National Standards Institute / National Information Standards Organization specification Z39.48-1992 (Permanence of Paper). It contains 30 percent post-consumer waste and is certified by the Forest Stewardship Council.

Library of Congress Cataloging-in-Publication Data

Driskell, Boyce N.
Tuckaleechee Cove : a passage through time / Boyce N. Driskell and Robert J. Norrell. — First edition.
pages cm
Includes bibliographical references and index.
ISBN 978-1-62190-167-9 (pbk.)
1. Cherokee Indians—Tennessee—Townsend Region—History.
2. Cherokee Indians—Tennessee—Townsend Region—Antiquities.
3. Townsend Region (Tenn.)—History.
I. Norrell, Robert J. (Robert Jefferson)
II. Title.

E99.C5D79 2015
976.8'885—dc23 2014038347

CONTENTS

ILLUSTRATIONS

Figures

Tables

Plates

PREFACE

Beginning in 1999, archaeologists from the University of Tennessee's Center for Transportation Research Archaeological Studies Group (UT-CTRASG) conducted archaeological investigations in association with the widening of State Routes 73 (US 321) and 337 from the four-lane section at Kinzel Springs to the Great Smoky Mountains National Park in Townsend, Tennessee. The project area is located in the western part of Tuckaleechee Cove in eastern Blount County within the Blue Ridge Physiographic Province. The total project length was 4.9 miles, encompassing field investigations of about 175 acres. The project was sponsored by the Tennessee Department of Transportation and the Federal Highway Administration.

The inspiration for this book came from the group of individuals who consulted to create the 2001 Memorandum of Agreement (MOA), as amended in 2003, among the Federal Highway Administration, the Tennessee State Preservation Officer, and the Advisory Council on Historic Preservation for the State Route 73 (US 321) Highway Improvement Project. These individuals included representatives from the Federal Highway Administration (FHWA), the State Historic Preservation Officer (SHPO), the Advisory Council on Historic Preservation (ACHP), the Tennessee Department of Transportation (TDOT), the Tennessee Division of Archaeology (TDOA), the Eastern Band of Cherokee Indians (EBCI), and the Chickasaw Nation. Other concurring parties to the agreement included the Tennessee Commission on Indian Affairs, the Great Smoky Mountains Heritage Center, and the University of Tennessee.

In addition to outlining a program of field and laboratory study of archaeological remains within the project area, this group mandated the creation of a version of the scientific results of the study that would appeal to the general public. Through several drafts, and informed by technical analyses and reports produced during the project (Boyce Driskell, *Introduction to the Archaeology of Tuckaleechee Cove, Blount County, Tennessee* [2011]; Elizabeth Kellar DeCorse, John F. Kvach, Robert J. Norrell, and Gail L. Guymon, *Euro-American Settlement in Tuckaleechee Cove, Blount County, Tennessee* [2011)]; John Marcoux, *The Cherokees of Tuckaleechee Cove* [2010], also published as University of Michigan Museum of Anthropology Memoir 52; Shannon D. Koerner and Lynne P. Sullivan, *The Mississippian Period Occupation of Tuckaleechee Cove, Blount County, Tennessee* [2011]; and Kandace D. Hollenbach and Stephen J. Yerka, *Archaic And Woodland Occupations in Tuckaleechee Cove, Blount County, Tennessee* [2011]), this book has evolved to fulfill that mandate.

The prehistory and history of Tuckaleechee Cove presented in this book are based largely on the large-scale excavations of archaeological materials from four of the sites investigated near Townsend. Nestled along the south bank of the Little River, Site 40BT89 (Kinzel Springs Site) is to the west and separated from Site 40BT90 (Apple Barn Site) by a small ridge spur extending almost to the southern bank of the river. Sites 40BT90 and 40BT91 (Pony Ride Site), to the east, are contiguous or nearly so, occupying parts of the same landform. These two sites are separated rather arbitrarily by a modern-day driveway.

Site 40BT94 (Gas Company Site) is farther to the east-southeast along the highway corridor, separated from the other sites by a rather broad hill spur that originally extended nearly to the southern bank of the river. Although similar in some ways but different in others, these sites are generally lumped together and are referred to in this book as the Big Dig, in reference to the massive amount of field excavations and analysis required to recover, process, and interpret archaeological materials in the construction right of way.

The fieldwork was performed for the Tennessee Department of Transportation (Project No. 05006-1238-04) through a contract with the general engineer, TRC (Project No. 98537). During this period, Charles (Chuck) Bentz initially served as archaeologist in general charge (principal investigator) under Tennessee Division of Archaeology Permit No. 000314 but was replaced towards the conclusion of fieldwork by George (Nick) Fielder, then state archaeologist and director of the Tennessee Division of Archaeology.

One of the authors, Boyce Driskell, took over the role of archaeologist in general charge of the Townsend Project in April 2002 during the very initial phases of laboratory processing. As director of the newly organized Archaeological Research Laboratory (ARL)—charged with the responsibility to process, analyze, and interpret the 1,200 boxes (cubic feet) of artifacts, thousands of field maps and drawings, reams of field documents and thousands of float and other samples—he organized research teams to generate the necessary data, analyze these data, and produce interpretations.

A "database" team, led by Nick Herrmann and ably assisted by Stephen Yerka, was responsible for developing a system to record, house, and organize the Townsend Project information. With the help of Rod Riley of IBM, a relational database was designed that allowed analysts to record artifact and other data directly into the database through a web-based interface available at each work station. Spatial data, including thousands of field maps, were geo-referenced and entered into an ArcGIS database. As another part of its duties, the database team assessed and assigned a temporal/cultural affiliation (TCA) for each provenience unit excavated and recorded at the Townsend sites.

Materials from well-preserved deposits that produced datable artifacts (ceramics, projectile points, beads, and so on) and/or dated samples (including C14 samples) were assigned TCAs, reflecting placement into a cultural period. Others were assigned to more general categories such as "prehistoric" or "Archaic." Because of extensive plowing and other disturbances from two hundred years of EuroAmerican utilization of the Townsend sites, archaeological deposits were generally poorly preserved. Intact deposits were found only in a few small areas beneath the plow zone. Most of the intact deposits came from the 3,395 features and thousands of postholes that were preserved in the sterile deposits beneath the plow zone. For this reason, most of the analyses conducted on materials from the Townsend sites focused on the contents and context of features like pits, postholes, and houses.

After initial processing, so-called "period" teams began the arduous task of data analysis, interpretation, and writing of the cultural-historical interpretative reports. The Euro-American analysis team was originally led by Todd Ahlman, followed by Elizabeth Kellar DeCorse. Dr. DeCorse wrote most of the archaeological report and generally supervised the production of the report. John Kvach and Professor Jeff Norrell from UT's Department of History prepared the first part of the volume on the history of Tuckaleechee Cove, while Gail Guymon of the Archaeological Research Laboratory prepared the second part on land tenure in the cove.

The Cherokee period team was led by Brett H. Riggs, research archaeologist at the Research Laboratories of Archaeology at the University of North Carolina, Chapel Hill, who along with Jon Marcoux, a PhD candidate at UNC, Chapel Hill, at that time, collaborated with the Archaeological Research Laboratory on the research and writing of this volume.

The Mississippian period team was headed by Lynne Sullivan, curator at the McClung Museum, University of Tennessee, who, along with Shannon Koerner, a PhD candidate in the Anthropology Department at the University of Tennessee, collaborated with the Archaeological Research Laboratory on the research and writing of the volume on the Mississippian period in Tuckaleechee Cove.

The Archaic/Woodland period team was led by Kandace Hollenbach, research associate professor and laboratory director for the Archaeological Research Laboratory, who along with Stephen Yerka, a PhD student in the Anthropology Department and IT manager for the Archaeological Research Laboratory at the University of Tennessee, organized the research and reporting found in the volume on the Archaic and Woodland periods in Tuckaleechee Cove.

The research into Townsend ceramics reported in this volume was greatly facilitated by the ARL ceramics team, led first by Todd Ahlman, then by Scott Hammerstedt, and ably assisted by Cameron Howell. Plant and animal remains recovered during the archaeological investigations were analyzed by the subsistence team led by Kandace Hollenbach. The lithics team led by Boyce Driskell analyzed and reported the stone artifacts, including tools and the stone debris left from their manufacture.

After fieldwork was completed, three of the excavation supervisors—Mike Angst, Bradley Creswell, and Cameron Howell—provided other analysts with insight into notes, maps and photographs from the project.

Funding for the project was provided by the Federal Highway Administration and the Tennessee Department of Transportation. Thanks are in order to these agencies for providing the funds to support the project through its fourteen-year history. These agencies also directed the process of establishing the MOA, which provided an overall plan for the project.

The Eastern Band of Cherokee Indians played a central role in the consultation process. This was particularly the case in dealing with the 104 human burials found during the excavations.

Since the EBCI opposed removal of the burials, a compromise was reached in which burials were left in place and undisturbed, and these features were not excavated out of respect for the spirits of their ancestors. Special arrangements were made to protect each burial within the project area from construction damage.

Gerald Kline, TDOT archaeology program manager, served as the TDOT archaeological manager of the project for the entirety of the project. He ably steered this project from the early days of project planning through the steps necessary to finish the research and reporting. Mr. Kline offered detailed comments and sage advice during the production of both the technical reports and this book.

Thomas Wells, Emily Huckabay, and Gene Adair, UT Press staff members, provided excellent editorial suggestions and corrections. Michael Aday, Great Smoky Mountains National Park Librarian-Archivist, and Kyle Hovious, UT Hodges Library special collections, were very helpful by providing high resolution digital images of historical photographs included in this volume. Bob Patterson and other staff members of the Great Smoky Mountains Heritage Center in Townsend provided the authors unfettered access to the Center and their collections.

The Townsend Project, by any measure, was a huge undertaking, involving hundreds of participants over the fourteen years since its inception. Any list that we might compile of other individuals we should thank would likely be inaccurate; however, about 250 people worked on the project at one time or another. All the participants in this project, including federal, state, and university participants, deserve our gratitude for their service, sometimes under trying circumstances. The authors wish to extend a sincere thanks to these unnamed individuals for their role in the process that made the insights presented here possible. Thanks are extended to all for the teamwork necessary to bring such a big and complex project to a successful conclusion.

The authors would also like to acknowledge the help of five anonymous reviewers who read and commented on drafts of the book. Any mistakes remain the responsibility of the authors.

BOYCE N. DRISKELL
Archaeological Research Laboratory

ROBERT J. NORRELL
Department of History
The University of Tennessee

TUCKALEECHEE COVE

Introduction

THE FACES OF TUCKALEECHEE COVE

Tuckaleechee is the name that Cherokees gave to an oval-shaped cove nestled within the western slopes of the Appalachian Mountains in East Tennessee. Millions of years of internal forces pushed the earth's crust upward, making mountains. Over time, erosion wore the mountains down and created rich pockets of valley land. Marked by steep mountain walls, flat river bottoms, and rich limestone soils, these oval-shaped coves range in size and elevation throughout East Tennessee. This book tells the story of one of them. Tuckaleechee Cove is oriented east and west and hooks southeastward to terminate in what is today the Great Smoky Mountains National Park. Its main geographic feature is the Little River, which, originating in mountain streams, flows westward, bisects the cove floor, and exits on the west. It then runs through Maryville and empties into the Tennessee River south of Knoxville.

Because of its geography, Tuckaleechee Cove forms a natural passage, or corridor, from the Tennessee Valley into the Appalachian Mountains. Beginning with the earliest humans to colonize the region some 13,000 years ago (or perhaps earlier), the cove has been utilized as a passageway into and through the mountains. People have used this important byway throughout the ages. Hugging the banks of the Little River, US Highway 321 is the most recent manifestation of this historical roadway.

Unlike earlier changes to the cove, the widening of US Highway 321 by the Tennessee Department of Transportation (TDOT) was accompanied by thorough archaeological and historical research to document the presence and nature of prior human occupations within the construction zone for the new highway and, more generally, in Tuckaleechee Cove.

Beginning in 1999, the archaeological investigations were undertaken to identify and determine the extent of prehistoric and historic archaeological remains within the route of the highway (plate 1). These investigations identified a number of concentrations of archaeological remains within an area about five miles long near the entrance to the cove (figure 1). Requiring nearly three years to fully excavate, these remains constitute the primary archaeological data currently known from Tuckaleechee Cove. In addition, historical records

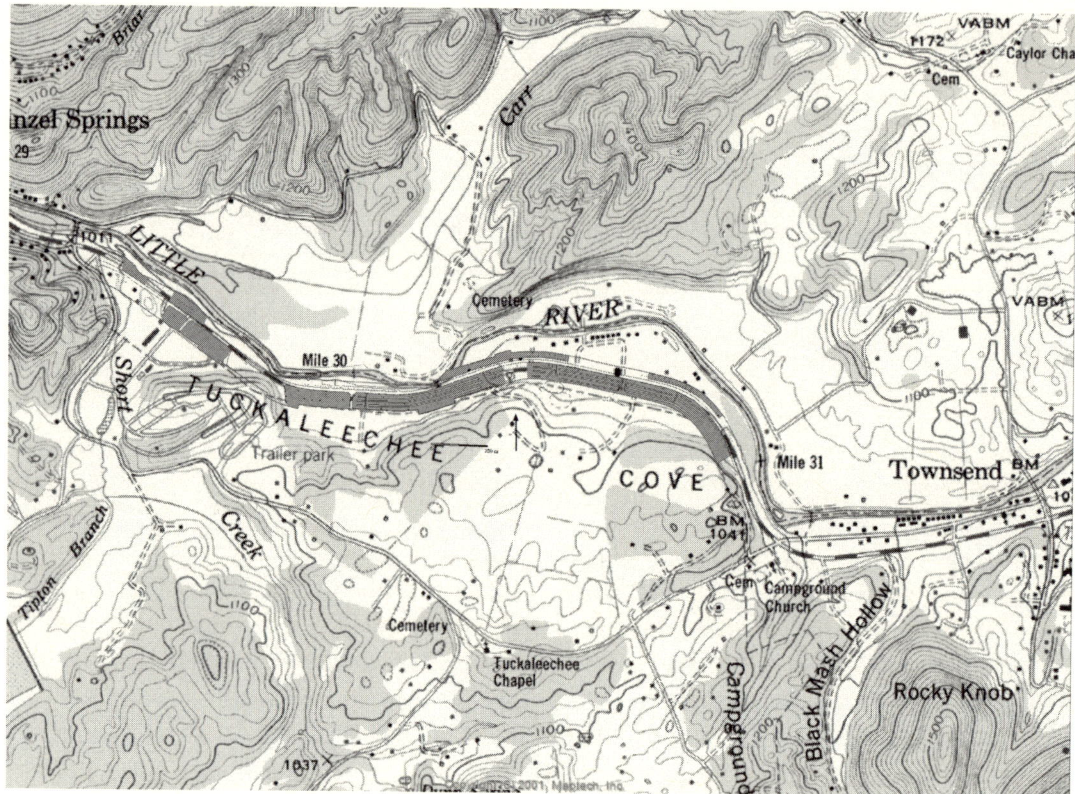

Figure 1. The Big Dig focused on an area within the right-of-way of Highway 321 from the entrance to Tuckaleechee Cove at Kinsel Springs eastward into the town of Townsend. (Staff drawing on US Geological Survey maps.)

were scrutinized as part of the project. Together, insights from the artifacts and documents (in essence "passages through time") inform this book.

Information collected during the project testifies to the presence of Native Americans in the cove for thirteen or more millennia. This beautiful land was home to Cherokees in the 1600s and early 1700s; EuroAmerican families settled in the late 1700s and 1800s. Each successive group created a way of life for themselves and their descendants.

People of the Cove

When the first humans saw Tuckaleechee Cove at the end of the Ice Age, more than 13,000 years ago, it looked much as it does today. It was colder then but warm enough for human habitation. Its geology and topology have changed little over thousands of years. The Little River's route through the cove has altered somewhat, and there are perhaps a few different plants today. It was more heavily forested, and its trees were more like those found in colder climates today, similar to those now at the top of the Smokies. In the Ice Age, fewer kinds of plants grew under the trees than grow today. The kinds of animals also changed. The mastodon, or American elephant, the giant beaver, and the large dire wolf became extinct at the end of the Ice Age. But most types of animals living in the cove at the end of the Ice Age have descendants there now. It was a beautiful place then, a good place to make a home, just as it is now.

The people who made Tuckaleechee Cove their home so many years ago, however, could not have been more different from today's inhabitants.[1] If ghosts could speak, they would tell many stories of the cultural groups, all distinctive, that have inhabited the cove. None of these differences were the result of biology. The first people in the cove were of Native American descent who shared genetic characteristics with some ancient East Asian populations. But many of the families in East Tennessee today also share those genes through Native American ancestry. Regardless of genetic characteristics, the first person to see Tuckaleechee Cove many millennia ago was like us today in all physical and mental characteristics. Even so, this person would be astounded at meeting a modern-day resident of the cove. Each would find little in common with the other in areas of language, technology, and worldview. The stories in this book will help distinguish differences from, but also similarities to, the various peoples who have lived in the cove over the last 13,000 years.

The first residents of the cove left no written records. This part of the past is commonly called prehistory. But by leaving behind artifacts that archaeologists have found, their lives can be recovered through archaeological finds in the cove. This first part of this book, based on years of archaeological digging and study of artifacts, recounts the story of thousands of years of unwritten prehistory.

The Cherokees, the last of a long line of Native Americans who lived in the cove, left no written records, but archaeologists and historians say that they lived in the "historic era" because EuroAmericans recorded events that tell us about the Cherokees. Even for those Cherokees who never saw a EuroAmerican, white people affected their lives. They brought to Cherokee lands deadly diseases, new technologies, and ideas that eventually displaced the Cherokee community in the cove.

The EuroAmerican settlers who came to the cove after the Cherokee residents were gone left a rich written record of their lives in maps, deeds, wills, letters, church minutes, and newspaper articles. They too left an archaeological record that has been uncovered. In this book, written documents are combined with archaeological finds to draw as many conclusions about these inhabitants of the cove as possible.

Historians and archaeologists do not hear ghosts, but our sources, the documents and artifacts left by departed residents of the cove, give us hints about the lives that came before us. While these sources are never as informative as archaeologists would like, they do offer bits and pieces of the past that allow historians and archaeologists insight into past

1. One of the most accessible, readable accounts of the early peoples of North America is David Meltzer, *First Peoples in a New World* (Berkeley: University of California Press, 2009).

histories, cultural traditions, and innovations. The story told in this book depends largely on the archaeological excavations during the road construction project. This is referred to in this book as the "Big Dig."

The Big Dig

The stories of peoples of the cove could only be re-created through a massive amount of research. The prehistory of Tuckaleechee Cove remained hidden until 1999 when archaeologists from the University of Tennessee began to investigate sites discovered while the Tennessee Department of Transportation was widening US Highway 321 from Kinzel Springs to the Great Smoky Mountains National Park in Townsend. Once the importance of the archaeological sites was recognized, TDOT sponsored three years of archaeological and historical field research, followed by eleven years of laboratory processing and analysis. These studies yielded several scholarly reports, compiled by the University of Tennessee researchers, on the prehistory and history of Tuckaleechee Cove. Before the project, the archaeologists had hints about what they might find from earlier digs made in the 1970s from the nearby Tellico Reservoir on the Little Tennessee River, but only with investigation in the cove could they find out how people had lived there.[2]

The archaeologists focused their research on an area near the western part of the cove at Kinsel Springs. Their work required great care and intense concentration. At each site, they excavated and recovered bits and pieces from past lives.

Early in the field research, they dug exploratory holes (shovel test pits) into the earth to determine the nature and the depth of archaeological deposits (figure 2). Some areas within the project were then plowed to look for concentrations of artifacts that might give clues to the location of buried evidence from past residents' activities (figure 3). In the "plow zone," the top few inches of soil disturbed over the centuries by farmers' plowing, artifacts had often been removed from their original locations. The objects were still informative, but this jumbling of soil, rocks, and plant and animal material reduced their scientific value. The archaeologists scooped away the plow zone for careful study and then with shovels and trowels investigated what was below (figure 4). There they found many cultural "features," or places that contained artifacts, which remained where they had been left hundreds to thousands of years ago (figure 5).

These included post molds, the dark stains left when posts from ancient houses and barns were burned or rotted in place; fire pits and roasting ovens; holes dug for storage or disposal of refuse; and ancient human burial places.

Each feature was carefully measured and sketched before it was excavated (figure 6). At first, only half of the feature was removed to study what lay within and around it. The

2. Jefferson Chapman, *Tellico Archaeology: 12,000 Years of Native American History*, 3rd ed. (Knoxville: University of Tennessee Press, 2014).

Figure 2. Shovel test pits, small excavations where the dirt was screened to recover any artifacts, were placed at intervals along the exposed areas of the highway right-of-way.

Figure 3. Newly plowed transects were carefully inspected to find concentrations of artifacts suggestive of nearby archaeological features buried beneath the surface.

Figure 4. After the plow zone was removed with a smooth-bladed backhoe, large areas of the project were carefully inspected for features—post molds, fire pits and roasting ovens, storage pits, and ancient human interments—underlying the surface zone.

Figure 5. Careful cleaning of project areas revealed dark stains indicating the presence of ancient pit features. The parallel lines running from the bottom to the top in the left half of the photograph are plow scars.

Figure 6. All excavations, like this of a rock-filled pit (*above*), must be carefully documented with field notes, scaled drawings, and photographs (*left*).

archaeologists then excavated the other half, taking care to separate layers of earth within the feature. The earth fill from the feature was then sifted through fine-mesh wire to recover artifacts in the soil. Part of the soil was put in water to get tiny plant fossils to float, after which they were removed and studied. During the nearly three years of excavations at the sites in the cove, UT archaeologists investigated 3,395 features and 18,584 post molds. They studied 488,124 liters of soil from feature excavations, examined another 153,185 liters of soil from hand-excavated test pits, and processed 11,375 flotation samples. They discovered 104 burial sites but, at the request of the Eastern Band of Cherokee Indians and other Native American groups, did not disturb them. The Cherokees advised the archaeological dig along the way.

Soil removed from each of the excavations was placed in buckets and transported to a central pavilion where the soils were washed and screened through one-quarter-inch hardware cloth to find and recover the artifacts (figure 7). When completed, the dig produced over one million artifacts (table 1) that testify to successive peoples living in the cove for thirteen millennia. The archaeologists made thousands of photographs, maps, drawings, and reams

TABLE 1. ARTIFACTS RECOVERED FROM THE TOWNSEND SITES.

Chipped Stone Artifacts	251,130
Ground Stone Artifacts	4,088
Steatite Vessel Fragments	1,359
Fired Clay and Daub	150,304
Ceramic Artifacts	226,533
Worked Bone	7
Glass Trade Beads	228
EuroAmerican Historic Artifacts	13,269
Mica Fragments	2769
Fire Cracked Rock	776,089
Total	**1,425,776**

of notes to accompany the artifacts and samples brought back to the University of Tennessee's Archaeological Research Laboratory. Teams of scholars, 150 in all, studied the artifacts.[3] But these studies only scratch the surface, so to speak, of the potential for information from the collections now stored at the University of Tennessee. Researchers for years to come will consult the artifacts, samples, and field notes from the Big Dig in Tuckaleechee Cove.

What kinds of things did the archaeologists find? From prehistoric times, the largest number of artifacts comprised items of chipped stone, which are easily preserved in the temperate climate of eastern North America. Readers will know such artifacts from having seen spear points and arrowheads. But the Big Dig recovered only about two thousand projectile points. Most stone artifacts were other tools or the debris from the manufacture of stone tools. About four thousand stone artifacts were pieces of stone vessels, many made of steatite, often called soapstone.

The second largest category of artifacts comprised pieces of prehistoric ceramic vessels. Ceramics are almost as long lasting as stone because after each vessel was formed from clay, it was fired to make it hard and water resistant. Another 150,000 pieces of fired clay were also identified. Some of these specimens came from clay that was heated at campfires, hearths, or fire pits, but most came from the walls of Native Americans' houses, where it was mixed with grass and small twigs and then plastered to the wall to create a smooth, secure exterior. Clay-daubed houses often burned accidentally, or perhaps were intentionally set on fire either because they were infested with vermin or to make way for new structures.

3. See Thomas W. Neumann, Robert M. Sanford, and Karen G. Harry, *Cultural Resources Archaeology: An Introduction* (Plymouth, UK: AltaMira Press, 2010), for an overview of the process of archaeological exploration and evaluation required by federal laws governing disturbance of archaeological remains on federal property or by projects supported by federal funds or permits.

Figure 7. All excavation fill was placed in buckets and moved to this pavilion, where it was washed and screened through hardware mesh to recover artifacts.

When such a structure burned, the clay daub on its walls was unintentionally "fired" like pottery and thus became much more resistant to dissolution in the cove's environment.

The archaeologists at the Big Dig were baffled to find only seven bone artifacts—apparently because the soils in this area are not conducive to bone preservation. They discovered some mica, an important material for making decorative ornaments, but each artifact literally fell apart in the field. Among the most interesting artifacts from historic times include 228 glass trade beads of European manufacture found near Cherokee house ruins. Since these date to the 1600s and 1700s, they represent artifacts traded to the Cherokees prior to the arrival of EuroAmericans in Tuckaleechee Cove.

After fourteen years of study by University of Tennessee archaeologists and historians, the stories unearthed during the Big Dig in Tuckaleechee Cove can be told. Historians and archaeologists normally write books and articles for other scholars, and indeed our research findings have been reported in five lengthy scientific volumes with much technical detail. But in this book, we attempt to summarize the results of research in nontechnical terms for the general reader.

Our stories come with a minimum of interruption for citations, though when compelled to reference words and thoughts, we have added footnotes. These notes cite other scholarly works that may be of interest. At the end of each chapter, a few suggested readings of possible interest to the general reader are also listed.[4]

Telling the Stories

The first people of Tuckaleechee Cove described below are the early, prehistoric human bands of hunters and collectors, or foragers, as archaeologists often call them, from about 13,000 years ago or somewhat earlier. But recently archaeologists have found some intriguing evidence that human antiquity in the New World extends back much further. Who were these earlier people? Did they visit or live in the cove? While we may never know the true antiquity of humans in Tuckaleechee Cove, archaeologists will continue to search for new evidence.

To assist readers in placing the stories in sequence, table 2 presents a timeline of peoples in the cove. Chapter 1 introduces the earliest known Tuckaleechee Cove residents, the ancient foragers of the Paleoindian and Archaic periods. In chapter 2, we tell the story of Skittletown, a fortified, Native American village that dates to about 1,700 to 1,000 years ago. Skittletown's story is about farmers, people descended from foragers of the earlier era but quite different from them. Chapter 3 recounts the story of the Cherokees in the 1600s and 1700s. Although sharing an ancestry and many cultural traditions, each group of Native Americans in the cove was distinctive. The first two accounts of inhabitants of the cove are based entirely on archaeological research, but in the case of the Cherokees, both archaeological information and historical documents are used to describe the Cherokee presence in Tuckaleechee Cove.[5]

In chapter 4, EuroAmericans enter the cove as hunters, explorers, and traders and later as settlers looking for farmland for themselves and their families. The American Civil War and its aftermath, recounted in chapter 5, punctuates this story of the development of EuroAmerican culture in the cove. After the war came the tides of economic change and "progress." In our final story, recounted in chapter 6, the people of the cove remake themselves as capitalists, industrialists, and, eventually, hosts to the many tourists who visit what is now called the "Peaceful Side of the Smokies."

This book concludes in chapter 7 with a mention of recent developments in the cove involving heritage tourism and the contributions of the Tennessee Department of Transportation

4. Technical reports (see preface) for the Townsend Archaeological Project were prepared for the Federal Highway Administration and the Tennessee Department Of Transportation, Nashville, Tennessee. Jon Marcoux completed a doctoral dissertation on the Cherokee remains from the Townsend sites entitled "Cherokee Households and Communities in the English Contact period, A.D. 1670–1740" (Dept. of Anthropology, University of North Carolina, Chapel Hill, 2008). Three master's theses within the Department of Anthropology, University of Tennessee, were also written on data from the Townsend Archaeological Project, including Edward William Wells III, "Soapstone Vessel Chronology and Function in the Southern Appalachians of Eastern Tennessee" (2006); Phyllis S. Rigney, "Usewear Analysis of Flake Tools from the Townsend Project (Sites 40BT89, 40BT90, 40BT91 and 40BT94), Blount County, Tennessee" (2009); and Jeremy L. Sweat, "Lithic Resource Survey of the Upper Little River Drainage: Raw Material Availability and Use at the Townsend Sites" (2009).

5. Jon Marcoux has also published *Pox, Empire, Shackles, and Hides: The Townsend Site, 1670–1715* (Tuscaloosa: University of Alabama Press, 2010), in which he summarizes research into the Cherokees of Tuckaleechee Cove.

TABLE 2. TIME PERIODS FOR TUCKALEECHEE COVE.

	Cultural Groups	Years before present
Hunters and Gatherers to Horticulturalists	before Paleoindian Period	>13,000 years ago
	Paleoindian Period	13,000 to 10,000 years ago
	Early and Middle Archaic Period	10,000 to 5,000 years ago
	Late Archaic Period	5,000 to 2,900 years ago
Horticulturalists	Early Woodland Period	2,900 to 2,200 years ago
	Middle Woodland Period	2,200 to 1,400 years ago
	Late Woodland Period	1,400 to 1,100 years ago
	Mississippian Period	1,100 to 400 years ago
	Cherokee Period	400 to 200 years ago
Farmers and Industrialists	EuroAmerican Period	200 years ago to present

in sponsoring the Great Smoky Mountains Heritage Center, a special destination for visitors to the cove. This discussion is followed by some concluding thoughts about the stories we have told and the journeys undertaken by the peoples of the cove, and current and future faces in the cove. We hope that this attempt to place the peopling of Tuckaleechee Cove into historical perspective, done with a keen eye for the changes that took place in population and society, will provoke some thought about people and time, and archaeology and history.

Suggested Readings

Edwards, Grace Toney, JoAnn Aust Asbury, and Ricky L. Cox, eds. *A Handbook of Appalachia: An Introduction to the Region.* Knoxville: University of Tennessee Press, 2006. This volume presents diverse discussions about people, history and developments in the Smokies.

Lewis, Thomas M. N., and Madeline Kneberg. *Tribes That Slumber: Indians of the Tennessee Region.* Knoxville: University of Tennessee Press, 1958. Although outdated on many details, this popular book, written for a general audience, tells the general story of the prehistory of the upper Tennessee Valley.

Gibbon, Guy. *Archaeology of Prehistoric Native America: An Encyclopedia.* New York: Garland Publishing, 1998. This hefty volume is a very informative and easily used reference to many topics in prehistory with short synopses in alphabetical order written by experts on each subject.

Chapter 1

ANCIENT PEOPLE OF THE COVE

Prehistoric people may have seen Tuckaleechee Cove 13,000 years ago, or even earlier. Certainly, people who made the rather spectacular Clovis fluted points were in the region, since these projectile points have been found near the cove.

A few artifacts found at the Big Dig hint at an earlier Native American presence in the cove than do most other artifacts found during the excavations. The earliest artifact, the Quad projectile point pictured in figure 8 dates to about 10,500 years ago. It is a Paleoindian spear point that came from the Big Dig but may have been more recently brought to the discovery location from somewhere else because no artifacts of similar age were found at the site. The absence of earlier artifacts from the Big Dig means that archaeologists must use evidence from other places nearby to tell the early history of the cove.

Based on a few finds in North and South America that suggest the presence of people far earlier than the Paleoindians, archaeologists are now investigating the possibilities of colonization of the New World as early as 20,000 years ago or earlier. Various theories of colonization from Asia and Europe have been proposed, but the most tangible evidence for peoples in Tuckaleechee Cove is that of the Paleoindians.

The First People in the Cove, 13,000–10,000 Years Ago

Archaeologists call the earliest inhabitants of our region the Paleoindians, and the first question they ask is: Where did the Paleoindians come from? Traditionally, archaeologists believed that they migrated from Siberia in eastern Asia across a land bridge that in the Ice Age connected Asia to North America at Alaska. This strip of land was covered with water when glaciers of the Ice Age melted. From there, it is speculated, the Paleoindians moved southward either through a corridor that was free of ice during the late Ice Age or down a now-submerged coastal plain off the north Pacific coast. Once they moved below the glaciers

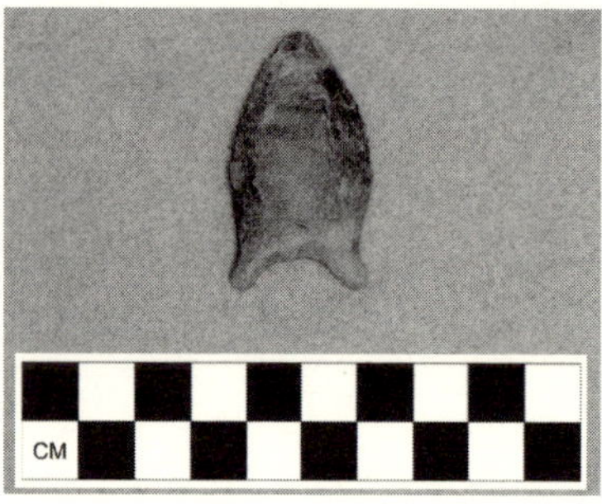

Figure 8. The Quad projectile point found at the Big Dig (*above*) and artist Greg Harlin's concept of a Paleoindian foraging band. (Artist image courtesy of McClung Museum of Natural History and Culture, University of Tennessee.)

that then covered what is now the northern tier of the United States, they fanned out to various areas, including the Appalachian Mountains.[1]

Archaeological evidence shows that Paleoindians sometimes butchered and ate large animals, including giant tortoises and mastodons, an Ice Age elephant species, before these animals became extinct around 11,000 years ago. Archaeologists do not know whether they hunted these animals or if they took advantage of some that were crippled or dying. The big animals were not reliable prey, because there were relatively few of them in the Appalachian area. The Paleoindians must have mostly eaten smaller game animals—deer, water fowl, and wild turkeys—as well as wild fruits, nuts, and seeds of weedy plants.[2] Paleoindian sites that might provide firm answers to dietary questions are rare, and those discovered do not contain the organic remains necessary to answer definitely the questions about diet. However, excavations at Dust Cave, near Florence, Alabama, revealed deposits protected

1. As noted above, Meltzer's *First Peoples in a New World* presents a very readable and balanced account of the current ideas about the early peopling of the New World.

2. Renee B. Walker's analysis of animal bone from Dust Cave revealed a distinct preference for aquatic species during the Paleoindian period. Her research is summarized in the chapter "Hunting in the Late Paleoindian Period: Faunal Remains from Dust Cave, Alabama" in *Foragers of the Terminal Pleistocene in North America*, ed. Renee B. Walker and Boyce N. Driskell (Lincoln: University of Nebraska Press, 2007).

by a cave environment that were laden with fish remains. This evidence suggests that the Paleoindians in southeastern North America were foragers, people whose living came from collecting, hunting, and fishing an array of natural foods.[3]

Because archaeologists usually find only the stone spear points and other stone tools associated with hunting, they often assume that hunting was the paramount activity of Paleoindian people.[4] In fact, it is very clear from anthropological studies of recent foragers that everyone in the society, based on age and gender, had important jobs to do. While men may have done most of the hunting, women, children, and elderly individuals probably spent most of their time collecting edible and medicinal plants. They may have been the fishers, and they probably set and monitored animal traps, including nets.

Many artifacts related to these important subsistence pursuits are not usually preserved because they were made of perishable materials. Without doubt, Paleoindians made baskets, nets for fishing and perhaps for catching birds or other small animals, and wooden tools such as digging sticks and clubs. Tools made of leather, wood, and vines no doubt existed, but such materials did not survive in the cove. Perhaps someday archaeologists will find evidence of them in special locations like caves where ancient organic material is sometimes preserved. While hunters provided valuable protein for the diet, others in the group probably provided the majority of calories consumed on a daily basis. After all, hunting alone is not a very reliable way of making a living since success is variable and unpredictable.

The Paleoindian people lived in small bands that probably included a nuclear family and some additional relatives. Archaeologists have not discovered permanent or substantial houses dating to their period, so it is assumed that they lived in temporary housing, perhaps tent-like structures. They may have moved regularly because even a small group of people could exhaust animal and plant resources in an area quickly. Some archaeologists think that Paleoindians exploited different ecological areas within a particular territory, perhaps staying in the same place every spring or fall. Others speculate that Paleoindians moved across broad expanses of territory. Stone tools from faraway geological sources are sometimes found at Paleoindian sites, which supports this theory. Leaf-shaped spear points and animal-hide scrapers that are similar in style are found all across North America, which is evidence that Paleoindian people moved widely and interacted regularly with other related groups.[5]

---

3. A good discussion of the patterns of prehistoric wild plant usage in the Eastern Woodlands of North America can be found in Kristen Gremillion's chapter, "Eastern Woodlands Overview," and Margaret Scarry's chapter, "Patterns of Wild Plant Utilization in the Prehistoric Eastern Woodlands," in *People and Plants in Ancient Eastern North America*, ed. Paul E. Minnus (Washington, DC: Smithsonian Books, 2003).

4. Noel D. Justice provides a very useful reference for projectile-point styles of the Eastern United States in *Stone Age Spear and Arrow Points of the Midcontinental and Eastern United States* (Bloomington: Indiana University Press, 1987).

5. Paleoindian and Archaic foraging patterns evident from the archaeological remains from Dust Cave, a site in northern Alabama, are described in Kandace Hollenbach, *Foraging in the Tennessee River Valley, 12,500 to 8,000 Years Ago* (Tuscaloosa: University of Alabama Press, 2009).

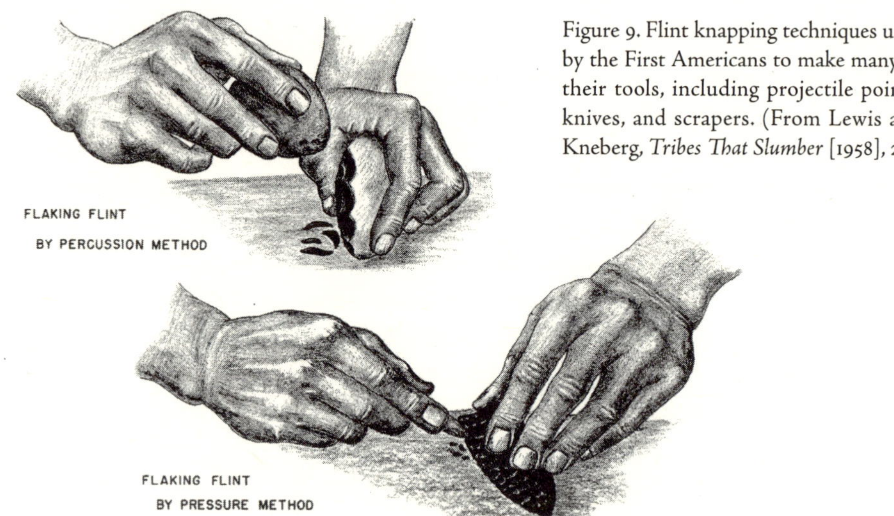

Figure 9. Flint knapping techniques used by the First Americans to make many of their tools, including projectile points, knives, and scrapers. (From Lewis and Kneberg, *Tribes That Slumber* [1958], 22.)

Proof of the presence of Paleoindians in Tuckaleechee Cove came with the discovery of the chipped stone projectile point (the Quad point, figure 8) dating from 10,800 to 10,500 years ago in a deposit of debris or garbage that archaeologists call "midden." A Cherokee household probably left it. This finding raises the question: Did Paleoindian people visit the cove, or did a later Cherokee occupant find the spear point at another place and bring it home to the cove? So far, archaeologists do not know the answer.

Stone artifacts of the Paleoindian period, including this projectile point, were fashioned through a technique that archaeologists call flint knapping (figure 9). In flint knapping, the maker used a hammer stone to generally shape other stones into the desired size and shape. Fine, detailed shaping was done by a technique called pressure flaking, in which the point of a deer antler was placed near the edge of the artifact and then pressure was exerted until a small flake was removed. Although flint knapping would seem to be a difficult craft to master, it was one that the First Americans brought with them to the New World.

Stone tools are often preserved on even the most ancient of archaeological sites. Archaeologists often find the debris from manufacture of the tools. With careful study, manufacturing debris can be as informative as the tools themselves. Archaeologists have learned to distinguish manufacturing debris related to the different steps in the tool-making process and to various methods of production of certain tools. This information allows archaeologists to determine where certain activities related to tool making took place. Through careful inspection of tool edges under powerful microscopes, archaeologists can sometimes determine how, and on what material, a tool was used.

Later Foraging People, 10,000–2,900 Years Ago

Even though the climate warmed after the end of the Ice Age at about 10,000 years ago, the Paleoindian descendants, called the Archaic people, continued to practice the foraging, hunting, and fishing lifestyle that had worked well for the Paleoindians. Archaic people typically established camps at places alongside rivers, where perhaps they came together seasonally in larger groups to share information, select mates, and conduct ceremonies. Archaic foragers also made smaller camps in high areas of the Appalachian Mountains. This suggests a settlement pattern characterized by a base camp complemented with distant camps for finding flint, collecting nuts, and hunting deer. This was the main pattern of Archaic life, but archaeologists have detected some variations among regions, especially in the types of tools used.[6]

The Big Dig excavated small pits and fire hearths used by Archaic people and found projectile points and hide-working and butchering tools. Hunting was clearly important, but as with the Paleoindians, much of their food came from collectable resources. Some pits seem to have been cooking ovens in which a fire was built and rocks were heated red hot; then the pits were filled with food and covered with grass and earth. This method cooked food in much the same manner as a Dutch oven. It resulted in literally tens of thousands of fragmentary, burned rocks that archaeologists refer to as fire cracked rock (FCR). More than 750,000 pieces of FCR were recorded and studied during excavation at the Big Dig. Some recent studies in Texas suggest that these earth ovens were used primarily for cooking vegetables, but this pattern may have been different in the cove.

However, discovery of pestles and grinding stones (figure 10) more directly reveal the importance of plants in the Archaic diet. Charred remains of seeds, nutshells, and animal bone were found in the ancient pits and campfires. Walnuts, acorns, and especially hickory nuts were important food sources. As Archaic foragers began to gather large quantities of nuts, they encountered a logistical problem. How could they store surplus nuts while they continued to forage? They solved the problem by digging deep pits for storage (figure 11). Nuts maturing in the fall were placed in these earthen vaults and covered with enough soil to discourage pilfering from animals until the food was needed in the winter.

Walnuts were consumed raw, but the other nuts had to be processed. Acorns were soaked in water containing fireplace ash to remove bitter tannins, and then the acorn meat was ground into flour and used to make bread. Archaeologists think that hickory nuts, collected in great quantity during the Archaic period, were smashed into pieces with a hammer stone. They were held in place on a "nutting stone," a rock with pits in its surface to hold the nuts in place (figure 12). The fragments of nuts, both shell and meats, were put in water in an animal-skin container or a basket waterproofed with resin or pitch. Next, small heated rocks were dropped into the container of water and hickory nuts. When the container's contents boiled, the oils within the nutmeats floated to the top. These oils were skimmed from the top and saved to cool into a nut butter that was used in cakes or mixed with seeds or dried meat to form a nutritious and tasty meal.

6. David G. Anderson, "Models of Paleoindian and Early Archaic Settlement in the Lower Southeast," in *The Paleoindian and Early Archaic Southeast*, ed. David G. Anderson and Kenneth E. Sassaman (Tuscaloosa: University of Alabama Press, 1996) posits settlement in small groups who meet occasionally with other related bands for social and ritual practices.

Figure 10. Drawing of a grinding slab and pestle (*above*) alongside a grinding slab recovered from the Big Dig. (Drawing from Lewis and Kneberg, *Tribes That Slumber* [1958], 27.)

Figure 11. Large pits like this one from the Big Dig were created by Late Archaic people to store surplus foods, particularly nuts.

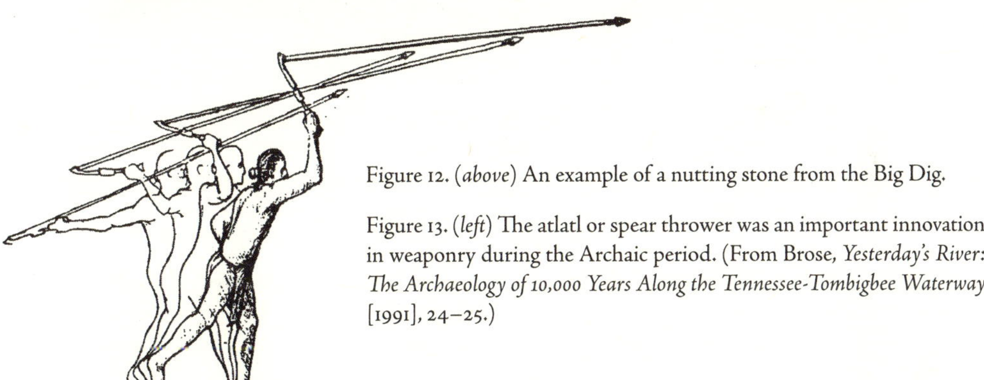

Figure 12. (*above*) An example of a nutting stone from the Big Dig.

Figure 13. (*left*) The atlatl or spear thrower was an important innovation in weaponry during the Archaic period. (From Brose, *Yesterday's River: The Archaeology of 10,000 Years Along the Tennessee-Tombigbee Waterway* [1991], 24–25.)

The Big Dig discovered hunting weapons used in the middle Archaic period from 8,000 to 5,000 years ago. Artifacts of the atlatl, a spear-throwing device (figure 13), were one important find. The atlatl was usually about three feet long, with a handle at one end and a hook at the other. A five- or six-foot spear was socketed into the hook, held with thumb and forefinger, and thrown using the atlatl as a lever, an extension of the arm. The atlatl multiplied the spear's momentum and distance and thus its killing power. In the hands of an expert hunter, it was a potent weapon. Weights were the most common parts of the atlatl found at the Big Dig; they were usually made of stone, which gave the device propelling power.

To produce an atlatl weight, the Archaic artisan first used a hammer stone to shape it (figure 14). To smooth and further shape the weight, the artisan rubbed it against a sandstone slab or with a hide to which a sand abrasive adhered. Chipped stone drills and hollow, sand-filled canes were used to put a hole through the atlatl weight and handle. The spears thrown by atlatls were tipped with projectile points made through the flint-knapping technique (figure 15, plates 9–14). A number of projectile points found at the Big Dig may have been spear points propelled by atlatls.[7]

The pecking and grinding technique was also used to shape stone axes such as the one pictured in figure 16. The groove facilitated a sturdy handle, probably made of wood.

The Big Dig discovered several small, flat cobblestones that were notched out on each side, probably by using another stone as a hammer. Archaeologists believe that these were used as weights, perhaps as sinkers for fishing nets. These artifacts suggest that fishing was important in Archaic and later prehistoric times. Bone was very poorly preserved at the sites, so this cannot be confirmed by recovery of fish bone.[8]

As was the case for the Paleoindian period, some Archaic tools were no doubt made of bone—typically awls for sewing leather, needles, and fishhooks. But these tools were rarely found at the Big Dig, probably because of decay. Even the most durable kinds of bone, such as deer antler, are rare in the collections from the sites.

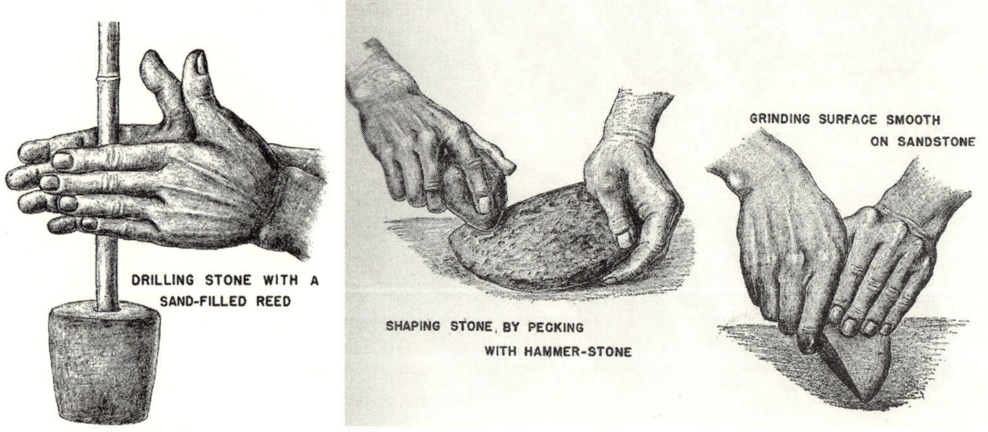

Figure 14. Steps in making an atlatl weight or other ground and polished stone artifact. (From Lewis and Kneberg, *Tribes That Slumber* [1958], 23, 27.)

7. The process of flaking a stone to produce a stone tool is described in detail in John C. Whittaker, *Flintknapping: Making and Understanding Stone Tools* (Austin: University of Texas Press, 1994).

8. See Boyce N. Driskell and Renee B. Walker, "Making Sense of Paleoindian Subsistence Strategies," in Walker and Driskell, *Foragers of the Terminal Pleistocene in North America*, for a brief discussion of early technologies and the archaeological record.

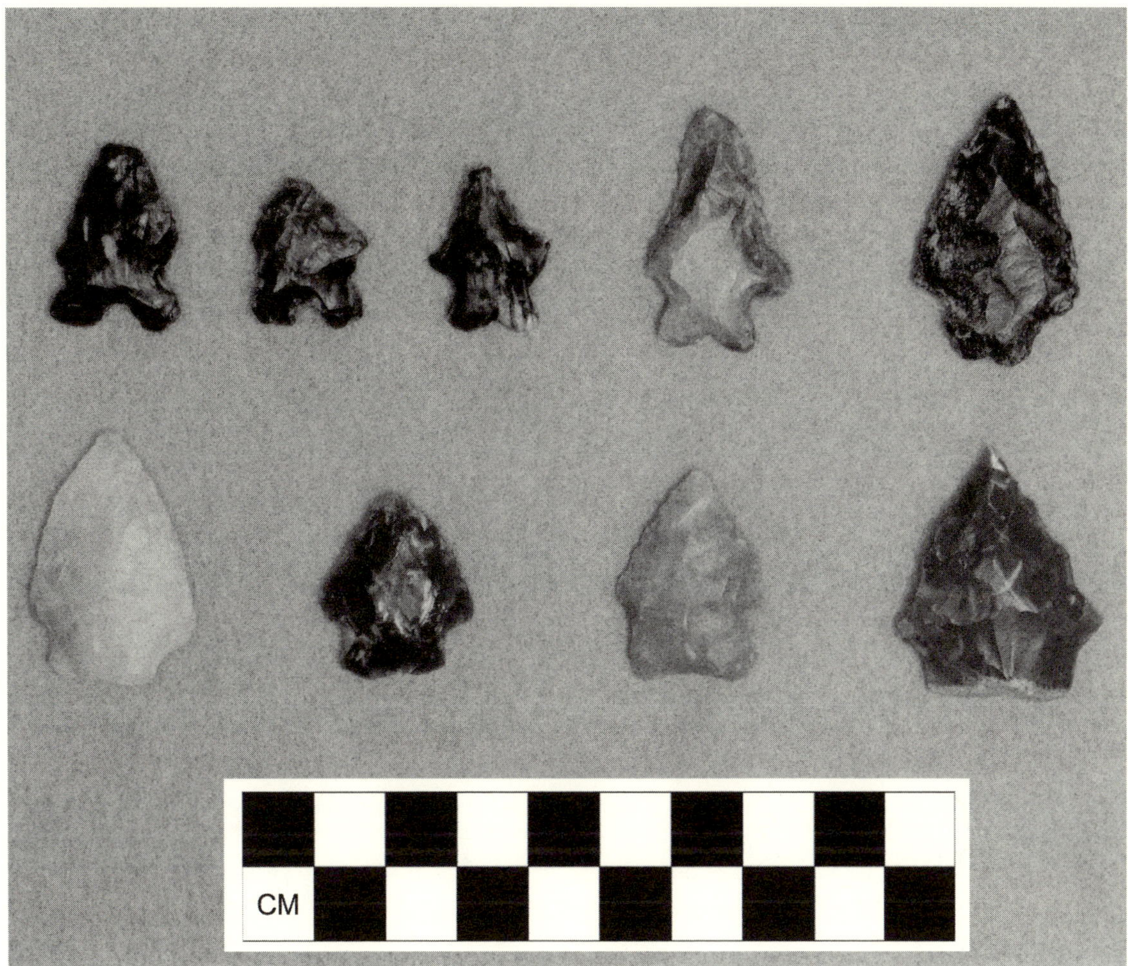

Figure 15. Early and Middle Archaic projectile points from the Townsend sites that might have tipped atlatl darts or spears.

Winds of Change

In the last 2,100 years of the Archaic period, from 5,000 to 2,900 years ago, the people became more settled. Their population increased greatly as they made innovations in food gathering and processing. They lived most commonly on the floodplains of rivers. They began domesticating plants and using stone cooking containers. The Archaic people of Tuckaleechee Cove began to trade articles with peoples of other regions. All these innovations characterize to an even greater degree the people examined in the next chapter.

Figure 16. A grooved stone axe, pecked, ground, and polished into shape from a river cobble, was probably attached to a wooden handle and used as a woodworking tool as well as a weapon.

Suggested Readings

Anderson, David G., and Kenneth E. Sassaman, eds. *The Paleoindian and Early Archaic Southeast.* Tuscaloosa: University of Alabama Press, 1996. Although technical and written for the professional archaeologist, this volume includes summary articles on early prehistory of various areas of the Southeast by noted scholars.

Gremillion, Kristen J. *Ancestral Appetites: Food in Prehistory.* Cambridge, UK: Cambridge University Press, 2011. This volume is a very good introduction into what paleoethnobotanists (a specialized area of study in archaeology) have learned about prehistoric foodways.

Chapter 2
THE FARMERS OF SKITTLETOWN

The culture of Native Americans that followed the earlier foragers described in the last chapter created a more complex society, one that probably engaged in more conflict with other groups. The evidence of wars rests on the existence of forts, called palisades, which were enclosures formed by rows of upright posts. Archaeologists believe the palisades discouraged raids and theft of food by other people and perhaps by animals. Several long rows of postholes found during the excavations at the Big Dig tell us of the presence of fortifications around villages and farms during the period from about one thousand to seven hundred years ago. Most of the palisades found at the Big Dig lasted from ten to twenty years, after which houses and food-storage "cribs" were often moved to another area along the Little River. Further excavations along the river would probably find more remnants of palisades.

During the Big Dig, archaeologists named one place "Skittletown," because the colored pie plates they used to highlight postholes for photographic purposes reminded them of a spilled bag of Skittles candies (plate 16 and figure 17). Archaeologists do not know what its ancient inhabitants called the place. At Skittletown the palisade protected several rectangular houses, made of wattle and daub. Wattle refers to wooden strips that are daubed with a sticky mixture of soil, clay, sand, and straw. Unlike at other sites, the palisade at Skittletown was rebuilt or repaired a number of times (figure 17), suggesting use of the structure for many decades. It also featured three semicircular extensions out from the main walls that archaeologists call bastions. Archaeologists believe the bastions provided stronger defenses for the people of Skittletown.

Who were the people of Skittletown? Who or what threatened them enough that they went to the trouble to build palisades around their villages? The answers to these questions take our story back at least two thousand years to the Late Archaic period in Tuckaleechee Cove.

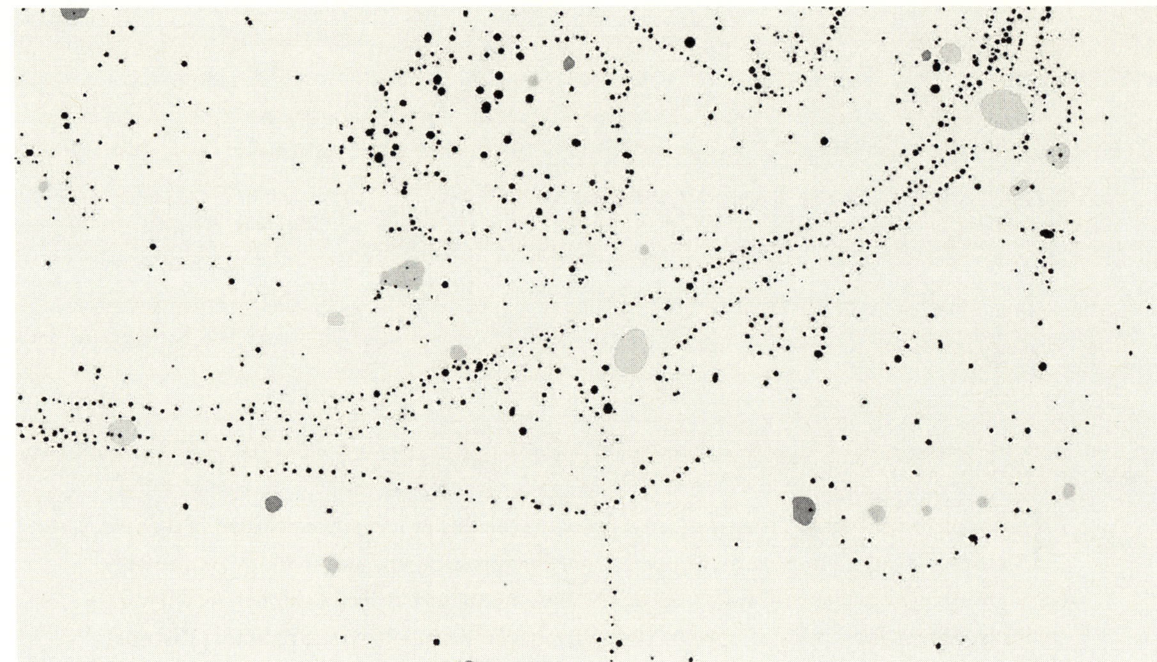

Figure 17. Map section of the southeast quadrant of Skittletown showing several lines of post holes defining successive protective palisades. (See also plate 16.)

Archaic Foragers Become Farmers, 5,000–2,900 Years Ago

After living in the Appalachian Mountains for eight thousand years or more, foraging people changed their lifestyle. Because change brings uncertainty about the future, people do not easily decide one day to give up a way of life they have been practicing for thousands of years. The lifestyle changes during the Late Archaic period were gradual, probably hardly noticeable at first. But once set in motion, changes in the way people acquired food became the spark that stimulated changes in daily life, housing, cooking, and even social organization. What prompted this change?

Archaeologists have found many Late Archaic sites, which suggests a population increase all across southeastern North America. These sites were larger and left more artifacts, the result of either longer or more frequent occupancy, or perhaps both. Population growth resulted no doubt from the success of Late Archaic foragers in Tuckaleechee Cove and elsewhere. Like their Paleoindian ancestors, the Archaic foragers gathered nuts and seeds; caught fish, mollusks, and waterfowl; and hunted deer, turkey, and small mammals attracted to the same nut, seed, and aquatic species. Populations living in a lush, resource-rich environment in a mild climate could grow rapidly. But as the density of the population increased, their home territories became smaller, and use of base camps for long periods increased.

Part of the explanation for change lies in geography. While nestled in the Appalachian Mountains, Tuckaleechee Cove provides a natural corridor into and through the mountains. Historians have documented the existence of an ancient Native American trail, originally referred to in the early part of the twentieth century as the "Great Indian Warpath"—in actuality a series of well-worn trails across the Southeast. A branch of the path ran parallel to the Tennessee River with another branch extending up the Little River into and through the cove and across the mountains to North Carolina. The map (figure 18) shows the routes of some of these trails. Knowledge of how to make pottery must have come to cove residents through these long-established transportation routes. Evidence of long-distance exchange during the Late Archaic period is the movement of steatite, or soapstone, into and through the cove. Other evidence comes from the presence of copper from the Great Lakes region and marine shells from the Atlantic and Gulf coasts in some sites in the region. Although archaeologists do not know exactly how their trading worked, there must have existed traders who either transported goods over long distances from their origin or, more likely, passed them along through loosely organized trading chains.

Steatite, which was sometimes used to make atlatl weights and other artifacts, was also the material used to make carved stone vessels during the Late Archaic period. Figure 19 illustrates a bowl similar to those used by people in Tuckaleechee Cove. About 1,300 pieces of soapstone, most from cooking vessels dating to the Late Archaic time, were left in refuse found at the Big Dig. Because there are no sources for steatite in the cove, soapstone vessels came from elsewhere, probably imported across the mountains from the eastern slopes of the Appalachians in the Carolinas and northern Georgia. Some of the decorative motifs on the steatite bowl fragments from Tuckaleechee Cove resemble decoration on bowls from areas as far away as Louisiana. Although they probably never ventured far from their home in the mountains, these people were part of a trading chain that extended from east of the Appalachian summit down the Little River and onto the Tennessee River into areas around the Gulf of Mexico.[1]

There are more questions than answers about the exchange of goods in and out of Tuckaleechee Cove in the Archaic period. Archaeologists know that stone bowls and perhaps other tools were brought in, but these researchers cannot say whether foods or animal products like deerskins or bearskins were traded. Archaeology answers many—but not all—questions.

1. Edward Wells III discusses the assemblage of steatite bowls from the Tuckaleechee sites in his thesis "Soapstone Vessel Chronology and Function in the Southern Appalachians of Eastern Tennessee."

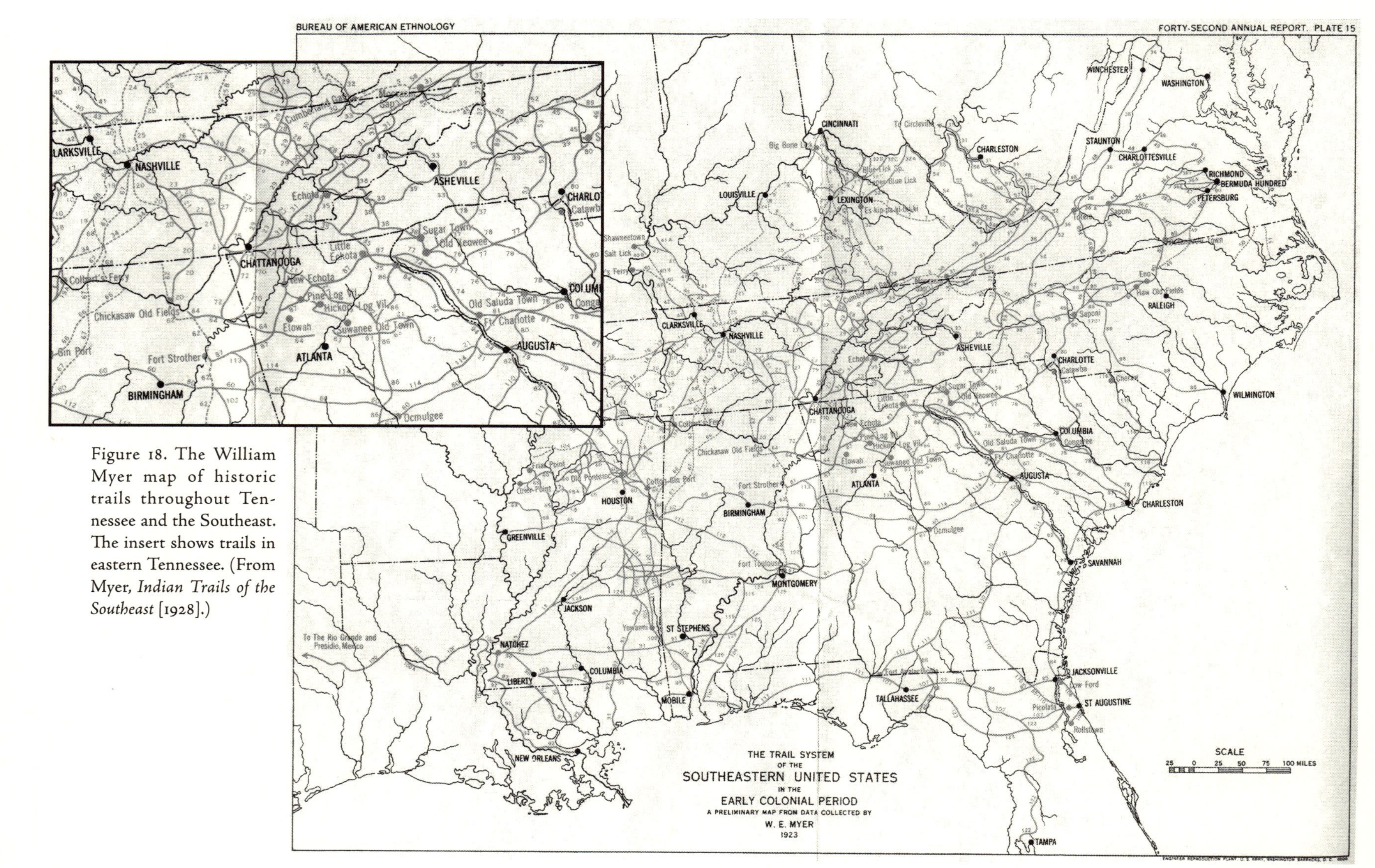

Figure 18. The William Myer map of historic trails throughout Tennessee and the Southeast. The insert shows trails in eastern Tennessee. (From Myer, *Indian Trails of the Southeast* [1928].)

Figure 19. A steatite stone cooking bowl similar to those found at the Townsend sites that is similar to the hundreds of steatite fragments like those from the Big Dig. (Courtesy of McClung Museum of Natural History and Culture, University of Tennessee.)

The adoption of steatite bowls represents a fundamental change in cooking techniques. Rather than dropping hot rocks into water, stone cooking vessels were placed directly on a fire. This change reflected the move to more permanent residence at particular sites, or at sites that were closer to each other. Stone bowls would have been too heavy and awkward for long and frequent moves.

Perhaps because of increasing population, the Archaic people began to experiment with growing food, instead of just moving around to collect wild plants. Archaeologists have found changes in the remains of squash and gourds, believed to have been used for food storage, which appeared in the region as early as about five thousand years ago. They believe that Archaic people selected seeds of preferred plants to sow the next season. By the end of the Archaic period, sunflower, goosefoot, and maygrass all were probably tended in native gardens. They all thrived in soil found in settlements of relatively big populations.[2]

To call these early plant tenders "farmers" would be misleading. They harvested native species that produced edible seeds in large quantities and then naturally reproduced the next year. These plants are easily harvested, and the most favorable seeds can be saved for planting

2. The so-called "Eastern Agricultural Complex" includes a group of annual plants native to the Midwest and eastern United States including squash, sumpweed, goosefoot, sunflower, maygrass, knotweed, little barley, and perhaps others that were domesticated by Native Americans for their seeds. For more information, see Bruce D. Smith, *Rivers of Change: Essays on Early Agriculture in Eastern North America* (Washington, DC: Smithsonian Institution Press, 1992).

the next year, thereby enabling selection to change the character of the plant species over many seasons. Such plant tending hardly interfered with the normal pattern of foraging life, at least not in the beginning. But by about 2,700 years ago, the occupants of Tuckaleechee Cove tended garden plots and planted little barley, maypop, bearsfoot, goosefoot, and other plants related to today's spinach, beets, and cucumbers. They dug storage pits for hickory nuts, acorns, and chestnuts. Perhaps not full-time residents of the cove, these predecessors to the Skittletown villagers probably returned there in spring and fall to sow and harvest their garden plants, gather nuts, and catch fish.[3]

Archaeologists believe that the earliest pottery was modeled after stone bowls like the ones found in Tuckaleechee Cove. Archaeologists on the Big Dig named the earliest, partially intact ceramic pot the "Ugly Pot." It was found sitting upright in a fire pit, and charcoal found in the pot dated to between 3,420 and 3,300 years ago. The Ugly Pot (figure 20, plate 2) had short legs to elevate and stabilize the vessel above the fire so that it would heat more evenly. The early dating of the Ugly Pot is intriguing, because it seems several centuries too old for the first ceramic vessels made in eastern Tennessee. Perhaps the charcoal found in the vessel was several centuries older than the pot itself.

Pottery making in eastern North America appears to have originated along the Atlantic and Gulf coasts as early as 3,500 years ago. Early pottery has been found also in the Upper Ohio Valley, where crushed rock and small flint flakes were mixed with clay. The Ugly Pot most closely resembles these pots from the upper Ohio Valley, but they date probably no earlier than 3,000 to 2,900 years ago. This suggests that the idea of pottery making entered the upper Tennessee Valley and the cove from the north-northeast instead of from the Atlantic or Gulf coasts.[4] Later Woodland cooking vessels from Tuckaleechee Cove looked like the one pictured in figure 21 and plates 3 and 4. The ceramic vessels pictured here are examples of only a few specimens that could be reconstructed from sherds (ceramic pieces) found at the Big Dig, but thousands of fragments testify to production of ceramics of various kinds.

As far as is known, pottery found at the Big Dig was made there, but vessel styles and decorations indicate influences from the Ohio and Tennessee Valleys, the Appalachian summit, and northern Georgia. In general, decorative patterns on pottery from the Big Dig can be found on ceramics from all parts of eastern North America, supporting the theory that technology and style were communicated through wide exchange networks.

---

3. Details can be found in Kandace D. Hollenbach, Judith A. Sichler, Jessica L. Vavrasek, and Jessie Duncan Johanson, "Late Archaic and Woodland Foodways in Tuckaleechee Cove," chapter 10 in Hollenbach and Yerka, *Archaic And Woodland Occupations in Tuckaleechee Cove.*

4. Fiber-tempered ceramic wares appear as early as 4,550 years ago in the lower Savannah River Valley and adjacent Atlantic coastal areas; these thick pots were often bowl shaped and were replaced later by more refined sand-tempered pots. See "Stallings Culture" in *Archaeology of Prehistoric Native America: An Encyclopedia, ed.* Guy Gibbon (New York: Garland, 1998). Another informative source of information on prehistoric ceramics of the southeast is Kenneth E. Sassaman, *Early Pottery in the Southeast: Tradition and Innovation in Cooking Technology* (Tuscaloosa: University of Alabama Press, 1993). Early Ohio Valley ceramics, appearing by about 2,600 years ago in the Lower Ohio Valley but perhaps earlier farther to the northeast, were generally thick-walled, conical in shape, and often cord-marked on the exterior surface. See Jon Muller, chapter 4, *Archaeology of the Lower Ohio Valley* (Orlando, FL: Academic Press, 1986), for a discussion of Early and Middle Woodland cultures of the area.

Figure 20. The "Ugly Pot," shown here in situ, is an early example of prehistoric cooking pots made and used by Woodland people in Tuckaleechee Cove. (See also plate 2.)

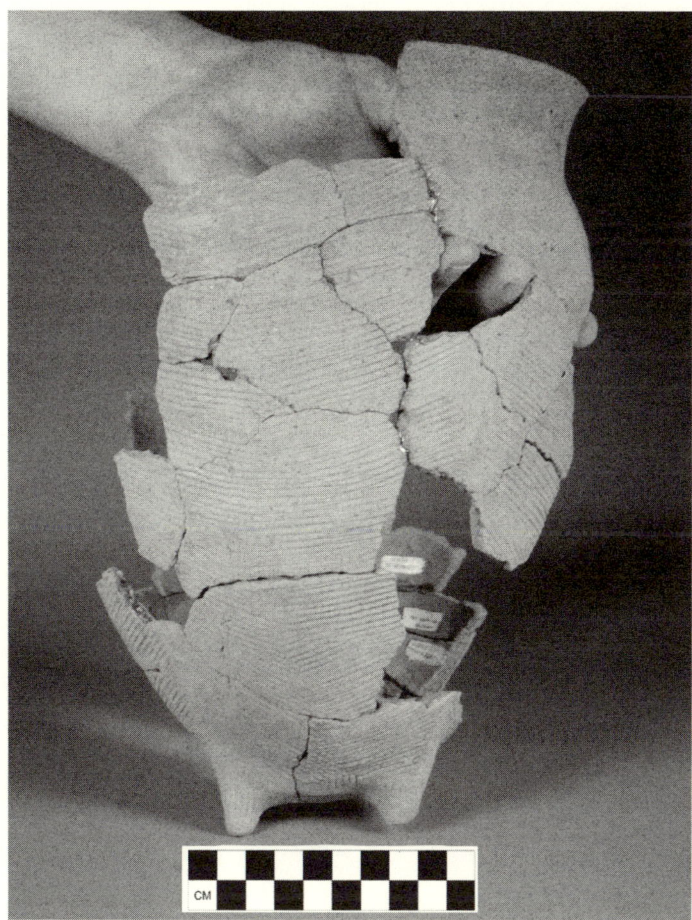

Figure 21. Woodland tetrapodal cooking vessel found during the Big Dig.

Woodland Horticulturalists, 2,900–1,100 Years Ago

Archaeologists have named the time from about 2,900 to 1,100 years ago the Woodland period, an era when Native Americans engaged in new farming practices, made pottery vessels, and built mounds to bury their dead. The change to the Woodland period was gradual; the people of the cove probably still gathered most of their food through foraging.

Prehistoric people in the cove kept dogs as pets and perhaps as work animals to flush, pursue, and corner game for the hunters. During the Big Dig, a feature was found that contained the completely intact skeleton of a dog (figure 22), indicating careful and intentional burial of a companion. Native Americans had domesticated dogs as far back as 8,500 years ago. Dogs were commonly buried during Archaic and Woodland times, often with artifacts and sometimes with humans.

Two sets of archaeological remains were identified at the Big Dig that date to Woodland occupation of Tuckaleechee Cove. The earlier group of Woodland remains date from about 2,600 to 2,200 years ago. The Woodland people used smaller food-storage pits, which tells us that they may have lived in Tuckaleechee Cove for most or all of the year. More evidence still was found for the period from 2,200 until about 1,400 years ago, when Woodland people made extensive use of the areas investigated in the Big Dig. Among many overlapping patterns of post molds, at least eight areas were recognized as remnants of houses. Many of

Figure 22. A dog burial excavated during the Big Dig.

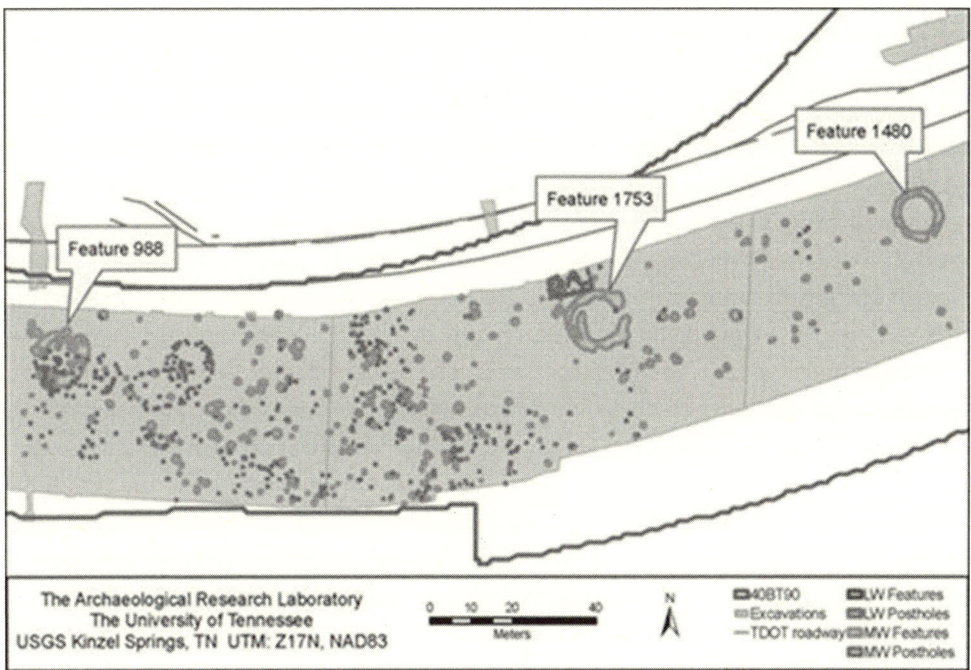

Figure 23. Three "circle middens" are probably small mounds that were plowed down over many years of farming the area.

these structures were apparently rebuilt several times and indicate that people probably lived there on a permanent basis. They continued to cultivate maygrass, squash, and knotweed and then adopted such new plants as maypops, tobacco, and corn.[5]

At the Big Dig, archaeologists excavated three circular areas of dark soil and debris (referred to as "circle middens"), which were possibly the remains of small earthen mounds (figure 23). Mound building began in northeastern North America during the Archaic period to cover and commemorate human burials. Similarly, mounds and raised earthworks have been found in the lower Mississippi Valley dating to five thousand or more years ago. These southeastern Archaic period earthen mounds were constructed as public areas, to create public and elevated sacred spaces for ceremonies and public buildings. Later, during Woodland times, many mounds in the Southeast were also built and used to cover and commemorate burials.

5. Judith A. Bense, "Woodland Stage: 1000 B.C.–A.D. 1000," chapter 6 in *Archaeology of the Southeastern United States: Paleoindian to World War I* (Walnut Creek, CA: Left Coast Press, 1994). For information about the prehistory of the domesticated dog in the New World, see Stanley J. Olsen, *Origins of the Domestic Dog* (Tucson: University of Arizona Press, 1985), and Darcy F. Morey, "Size, Shape, and Development in the Evolution of the Domestic Dog," *Journal of Archaeological Science* 19 (1992): 181–204. While corn is found in small quantities in Woodland contexts, it did not become an important part of the diet in the area until after 900 A.D. See C. Margaret Scarry, *Foraging and Farming in the Eastern Woodlands* (Gainesville: University of Florida Press, 1993), for a thorough treatment of prehistoric foodways in the area.

Combined with the evidence of permanent housing, the mounds suggest that Woodland occupants settled into permanent villages and towns. At least half a dozen Woodland residential areas have been recognized at the Big Dig, and reconstruction of individual houses suggest that permanent Woodland villages were established in the cove about two thousand years ago.[6]

The permanent houses and mounds tell us that the organization of society changed during the late Archaic and Woodland periods, although exactly how is an open question. Archaeologists know that social connections were no longer confined to small bands of close kin.

Now larger groups of inhabitants lived together in villages. Kinship still determined how individuals interacted, but authority became more structured. Some decorative symbols on artifacts, and particularly personal body decorations, may have related to identity in kinship, but archaeologists do not know enough now to interpret precisely what the icons mean. Later EuroAmerican explorers and traders sufficiently documented beliefs and traditions of southeastern Native Americans to the extent that archaeologists and anthropologists understand some of the basic elements of Native American kinship and social organization. Many archaeologists believe that these customs were deeply rooted and that Woodland people of Tuckaleechee Cove, and the prehistoric people who came afterward, thought in a similar way.

Matrilineal descent, or kinship determined by relation to the mother, was the dominant pattern in Tuckaleechee Cove. In this system, an individual's relatives include people, both male and female, on the mother's side but not those on the father's. Residence was usually in the mother's home. While the mother and the mother's mother were highly respected and honored, authority in the household usually resided with the mother's brother. Within the household, matriarchs were influential, but external power resided in the hands of a senior male member. All individuals who could trace their ancestry to one matriarch were part of a single lineage. A husband usually resided with his wife and their nuclear family, but his loyalties and responsibilities were mostly to his own lineage. Often several households in a village were part of a single lineage, but villages included more than one lineage and households of a lineage might be divided among several villages. A person without kin was a person without a home.[7]

Each lineage was part of a clan, a group of people that recognized common kinship but could no longer trace their relationship through a single known ancestor. Clan membership was the most important social identity of any individual. At the time of contact with EuroAmericans, Native American clans took the names of animals or elements of nature such as Bear, Bird, or Wind. The clan name was derived from a special association with the animal or natural element during its origin, such as identification of an animal that helped

6. For a discussion of mound building in the southeastern United States, see David Anderson and Kenneth Sassaman, chapter 3, *Recent Developments in Southeastern Archaeology: From Colonization to Complexity* (Washington, DC: SAA Press, 2012).

7. Charles Hudson, chapter 4, *The Southeastern Indians* (Knoxville: University of Tennessee Press, 1976).

Plate 1. Areal view of some of the excavations at the Big Dig in Tuckaleechee Cove.

Plate 2. The so-called "Ugly Pot," one of the earliest ceramic vessels found at the Big Dig.

Plate 3. This Woodland period Connestee tetrapodal ceramic vessel (specimen 00-2508-10) is the most completely reconstructed vessel from the Big Dig.

Plate 4. Partially reconstructed Woodland period check-stamped ceramic vessel (specimen 99-3554-467) from the Big Dig.

Plate 5. This polished stone artifact from the Big Dig was probably worn as an ornament or emblem (gorget) around the neck.

Plate 6. This chipped stone artifact, a prehistoric tool, was probably lashed or socketed into a wooden handle and used in a way similar to the modern-day adze to carve wooden objects.

Plate 7. The incisions on this stone object (lower right of the specimen) may depict a turtle.

Plate 8. Discoidal-shaped stones from the Big Dig. The right artifact is an intact example of a chunkee stone; the specimen left is a stone discoidal that might have been a chunkee stone or another type of gaming piece.

Plate 9. Most of these Early and Middle Archaic chipped stone projectile points tipped atlatl darts or small spears. The large projectile point to the right was more likely used as a hafted knife or as a tip for a handheld thrusting or throwing spear.

Plate 10. Late Archaic stemless and weakly stemmed projectile points. Technical type names include a–l, Guilford projectile points; m and n, Matanzas Correlate projectile points; o, Karnak Correlate projectile point; and p–r, Late Archaic Stemmed Correlate projectile points.

Plate 11. Late Archaic stemmed projectile points. Technical type names include a–d, Ledbetter projectile points; e, Pickwick projectile point; f and g, Appalachian Stemmed projectile points; h–k, Savannah River Stemmed projectile points; l–n, Flint Creek projectile points; o, Table Rock Correlate projectile point; p, Merom Correlate projectile point; and q–x, Terminal Archaic Barbed projectile points.

Plate 12. Early Woodland stemmed projectile points. Technical type names include a–k, Late Archaic Early Woodland Stemmed projectile points; l and m, Late Archaic Early Woodland Lanceolate projectile points; n–p, Saratoga Correlate projectile points; q, Cotaco Creek projectile point; r–u, Susquehanna Correlate projectile points; v, Adena projectile point; w–z, Dickson Correlate projectile points; aa–ad, Gary projectile points; ae–ah, Little Bear Creek projectile points; ai and aj, Robbins Correlate projectile points; and ak, a Kramer Correlate projectile point.

Plate 13. Middle Woodland triangular projectile points. Technical type names include a, Copena projectile point; b–f, Large Middle Woodland Triangular projectile points; g and h, Nolichucky projectile points; i and j, Narrow Middle Woodland Triangular projectile points; k–p, Broad Middle Woodland Triangular projectile points; and q–w, Middle Woodland Triangular projectile points.

Plate 14. Middle Woodland stemmed projectile points. Technical type names include a–i, Lowe projectile points; j–n, Narrow Thick Lanceolate Expanded Stemmed projectile points; o, Swan Lake projectile point; p and q, Narrow Thick Lanceolate Side Notched projectile points; r–u, Lowe Flared Base projectile points; v and w, Bakers Creek projectile points; x and y, Chesser Notched projectile points; z–ab, Steuben Expanded Stemmed projectile points; and ac–ah, Woodland Spike projectile points.

Plate 15. Mississippian arrowheads. Technical type names include a–j, Hamilton Incurvate projectile points; k, a Late Woodland/Mississippian Equilateral Triangular projectile point; l–s, Late Woodland/Mississippian Triangular projectile points; and t–cc, Madison projectile points.

Plate 16. (*above*) Paper plates indicate the postholes found at Skittletown. Note that red post lines define the protective palisade and yellow post lines define rectangular house areas. The smaller, round patterns denoted in blue are thought to be postholes from corn cribs.

Plate 17. (*left*) Cherokee period projectile points. Technical type names include a and b, Late Mississippian/Cherokee projectile points; c and d, Late Mississippian/Cherokee Ellipical projectile points; e, f, and g, Late Mississippian/Cherokee Lanceolate projectile points; h, j, and k: Late Mississippian/Cherokee Triangular projectile points.

0
5 cm

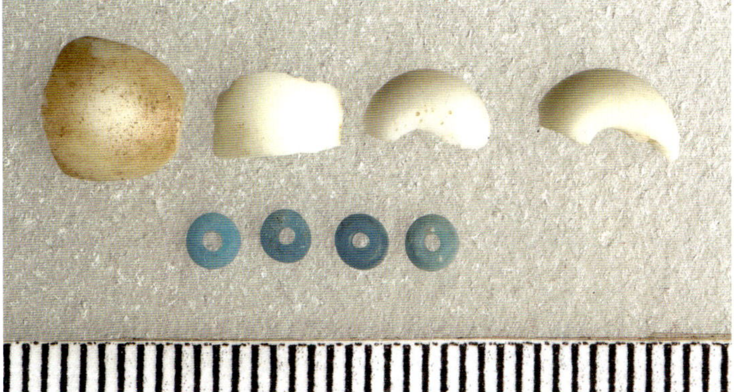

Plate 18. Collage of glass trade beads found in Cherokee homesteads at the Big Dig (tick marks indicate millimeters).

Plate 19. Historic artifacts found at the Big Dig. Artifacts include (from top left clockwise): a piece of a glass insulator; a whiteware plate sherd embossed with "ABCs"; two sherds of stoneware manufactured by William Grindstaff of Maryville; two clear glass bottle necks; a bottle glass sherd of a parent medicine embossed with "Dr. Pierce" (Ray Vaughn Pierce) of Buffalo, NY; redware ceramics and canning jar/lid liner fragments; and examples of transfer-printed ceramics.

the ancestors in a special way. Fellow clansmen could be found in many other places so that even if an individual was a total stranger to a local household, he was welcomed into the home of a fellow clan member. Marriage between members of the same clan was not permitted.

In the region around Tuckaleechee Cove, Native American groups were organized at the village and intervillage level into what anthropologists call tribes. When the word tribe is used in reference to American Indians, the average person often thinks of large groups, like the Cherokees or Creeks. In this sense, the term tribe generally refers to a group of people sharing a common language. To the anthropologist, tribe refers to an organizational level of society in which economic units, like households, occupied a contiguous territory and shared feelings of unity because of common traditions, habits, and language. They were united in a political system that might be temporary, such as the need to elect a chief to organize a war effort. Respected elders were usually called to serve in these temporary political offices. Anthropologists think that tribal organization represented more complex social and political associations than had existed earlier.

What does this mean for interpreting the Woodland remains from the Big Dig? First, if the circular middens are the remains of burial mounds, the people interred in each mound may have been individuals who occupied positions of high status in life. Archaeologists assume that artifacts placed in graves reflect an individual's status in life. As status differences became more structured and distinctive, burial placement and the goods put in each grave were good indicators of social status and wealth in life. Second, one post pattern dating to the Woodland period is that of a large, rectangular structure that probably served as a building for public meetings. This tells us that Woodland society in Tuckaleechee Cove was more structured than that of earlier cultures. If this building was a large house, it must have been the home of a person with high status.[8]

The grooved axes of the Archaic period were replaced in large part by celts, tapered stone tools with sharpened bits that were hafted into socketed wooden handles (figure 24). These tools were made from granitic rock that was pecked into rough shape and then ground and polished to produce a sharpened chopping tool and weapon.

Sharp stone scrapers and wedge tools used by people of the Woodland period were similar to those of the Archaic period (figure 25 and plate 6). Microscopic traces of wear found on some of these tools indicate that they were used on wooden objects like spear or arrow shafts. Other chipped stone artifacts were used to shape bone or leather or to punch holes in leather, bone, antler, wood, or stone. Stone wedges, when struck with a hammer stone, split wood and bone.[9]

---

8. Christopher Peebles was one of the first archaeologists to examine the burial goods from human burials as an indication of social status. His research into the burials at Moundville, a late prehistoric site in Alabama, popularized this approach to social analysis. See "Late Prehistoric Sociopolitical Organization in the Southeastern United States," in *The Development of Political Organization in Native North America*, ed. Elizabeth Tooker (New York: American Ethnographic Society, 1983).

9. Brian Kooeyman, *Understanding Stone Tools and Archaeological Sites* (Calgary, Canada: University of Calgary Press, 2000); Rigney, "Usewear Analysis of Flake Tools from the Tuckaleechee Project," 61, 74–76.

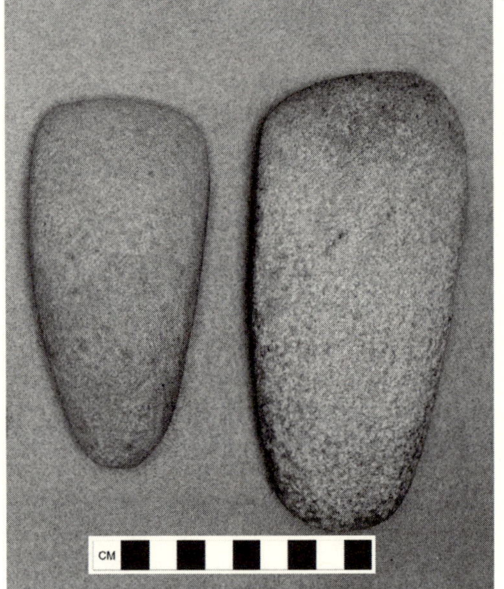

Figure 24. Ground, pecked, and polished stone celts or adzes found at the Big Dig. The tapered end was socketed into a wooden handle as shown in the reproduction. (Celt handle and photograph by Scott Hammerstedt.)

Near the end of the Woodland period, about 1,400 years ago, a revolutionary new weapon, the bow and arrow, was introduced (figure 26). This weapon changed the nature of hunting and warfare in long-lasting ways. Although the atlatl and dart (short spear) were accurate and forceful, the bow and arrow greatly increased the distance of the "kill zone" for both hunters and warriors. The bow and arrow was also a rapid-fire weapon in comparison to other prehistoric weapons; its user could quickly release a barrage of projectiles. Small, triangular arrowheads (figure 27), often made simply by altering the shape of a small flint flake with an antler pressure flaker, could be produced rapidly to replace broken, damaged, or lost projectile points.

Woodland people continued to use plants in the old ways, even as they developed new forms of agriculture. They still gathered nuts and wild plants, but they also invested more time in crop cultivation. They made grubbing hoes from sandstone and slate (figure 28) and planted goosefoot, squash, purple passionflower, and corn, though corn did not become an important dietary component until after 1,100 to 1,000 years ago. It is possible that early corn was either eaten green, leaving few traces in the archaeological record, or was served as a ritual food.

Woodland people created a pattern of long-distance exchange of goods, information, and religious paraphernalia during the first four hundred years after Christ. Archaeologists have named this system of exchange the Hopewell Interaction Sphere for the large Hopewell site in Ohio, which contained extensive burial grounds and seems to have been the center of the exchange system. There archaeologists found many artifacts made from materials that came from distant areas, from as far away as the Great Lakes, the Gulf coast, and the

Rocky Mountains. The way in which the interaction sphere operated is not known, but copper, silver, meteoric iron, obsidian, lead, conch shell, freshwater pearls, flint, and mica were exchanged in addition to artifacts made of these and other materials. Many artistic designs (icons) are repeated on the Hopewell artifacts, which are thought to represent important icons in the Woodland people's belief system. The interaction sphere was apparently

Figure 25. Bifacial scrapers (*a–d*), drill/perforators (*e–k*), hafted-end scrapers (*l–q*), and wedges (*r–y*) from Late Archaic and Woodland contexts at the Big Dig.

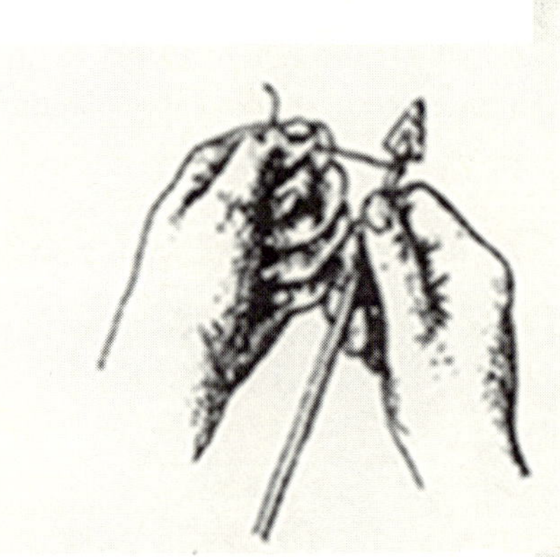

Figure 26. The bow and arrow was introduced to the Southeast about 1,400 years ago. The painting on the right is an early portrait (circa 1585) by John White of a Native American from Virginia. (© Trustees of the British Museum.) The drawing above depicts the attachment of an arrowhead. (From Brose, *Yesterday's River: The Archaeology of 10,000 Years Along the Tennessee-Tombigbee Waterway* [1991], 24–25.)

Figure 27. Small, triangular projectile points thought to be arrowheads from the Big Dig.

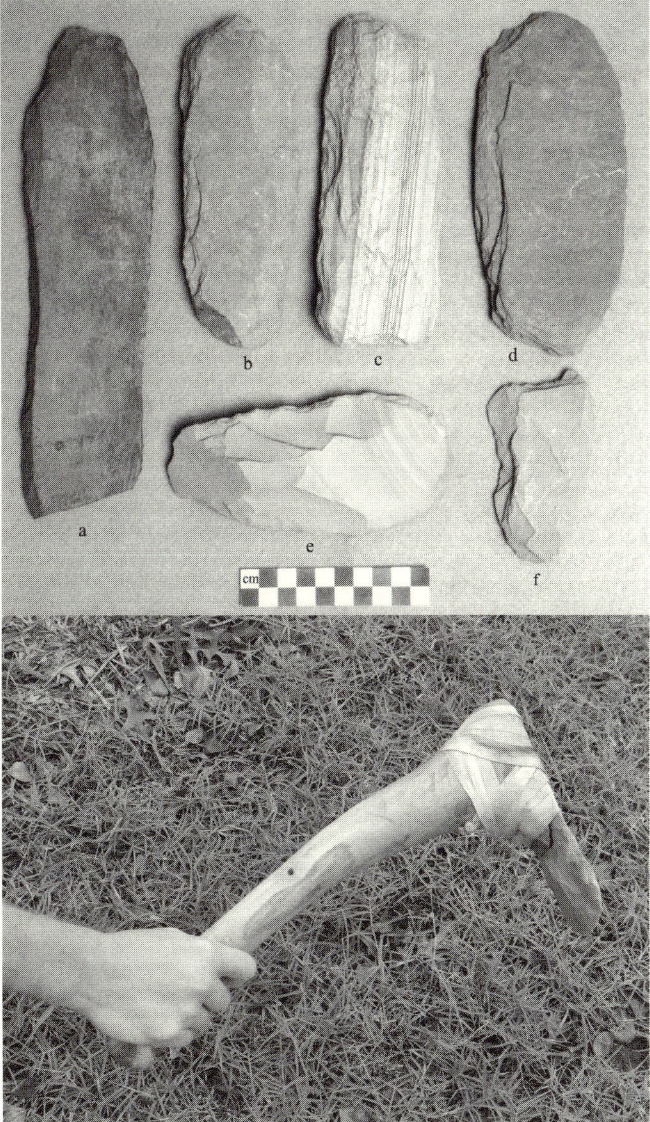

Figure 28. Hoes or digging tools from Late Archaic and Woodland contexts at the Big Dig. *Top:* Artifacts thought to have been used as hoes. *Bottom:* A reproduction of a prehistoric hoe by Scott Hammerstedt.

motivated by acquisition of exotic artifacts as important signs of rank and status; these artifacts were certainly desired as accoutrements in burials.

The villagers in Tuckaleechee Cove were probably part of or at least influenced by the Hopewell Interaction Sphere. The best evidence for this is the presence in the cove of a chipped stone blade of Flint Ridge Calcedony, the local flint of the Hopewell site in Ohio. Other artifacts that may have been influenced by the Hopewell Interaction Sphere include numerous pieces of mica recovered during excavations (figure 29), three unfinished artifacts thought to be pendants (figure 30), and a gorget (breast ornament) pictured in figure 31. Another gorget is shown in plate 5. The three mounds (circle middens) found during the Big Dig were possibly inspired by the Hopewell culture as well.[10]

The Mississippian People of Skittletown, 1,000–650 Years Ago

The Big Dig revealed that a somewhat different Native American culture, the Mississippians, resided in Tuckaleechee Cove from about 1,000 to about 650 years ago. Mississippian remains from the Big Dig reveal a series of farmsteads, spaced about a hundred yards apart, along the Little River. The farmsteads included one to several buildings, and curiously, each of them was surrounded by a fence or palisade (fortification) of upright posts. Single lines of posts in these palisades suggest that farmsteads were occupied for only about fifteen

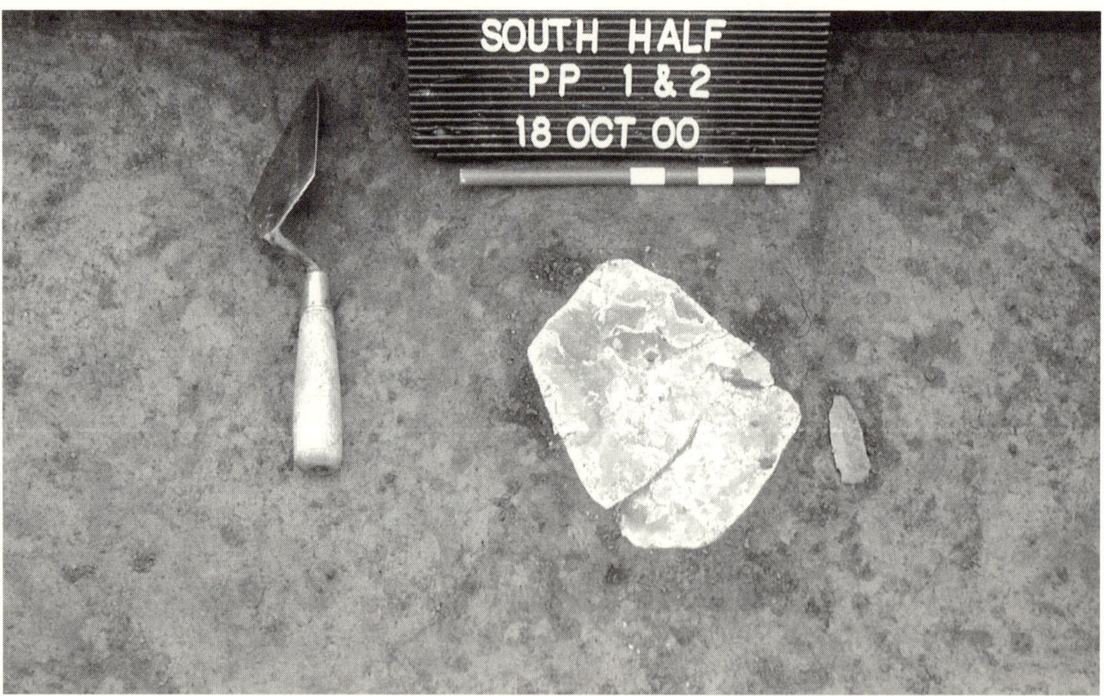

Figure 29. Cut mica suggests participation in the Hopewell Interaction Sphere.

10. Mark F. Seeman, "Hopewell Interaction Sphere," in Gibbon, *Archaeology of Prehistoric Native America: An Encyclopedia*; Mark F. Seeman, *The Hopewell Interaction Sphere: The Evidence for Interregional Trade and Structural Complexity*, Prehistory Research Series, vol. 5, no. 2 (Indianapolis: Indiana Historical Society, 1979).

Figure 30. *Left:* One of three unfinished (preform) pentagonal pendants from the Townsend sites. *Right:* Schist pentagonal pendant from the Pinson Mounds in middle Tennessee. (From Mainfort, *Pinson Mounds: A Middle Woodland Ceremonial Center* [1986], 69.)

Figure 31. *Left:* A gorget found during the Big Dig whose stylings might have been influenced by the Hopewell ideology. *Right:* An etching of the incised image.

years. Archaeologists have conducted experiments on the decomposition of upright posts and found that in most cases they were functional for ten to fifteen years—farmsteads were moved every so often to take advantage of fresh soils.

Near the center of this series of farmsteads was the village of Skittletown. Figure 32 illustrates the village layout and the location of the palisades in this fortified village. Note that the center of the village was destroyed when the old road was built in the 1950s, but seven structures were recognized. Two of these structures (1 and 13) are larger than others, suggesting their use as public buildings of some sort. Perhaps one was a chiefly residence and the other a public meeting house.

Figure 32 depicts the placement of at least four lines of posts in the protective palisade, indicating that the fortifications were rebuilt a number of times and that the village must have remained in this place for sixty or more years. These posts are on average larger in diameter than those in the farmsteads, suggesting more substantial fortifications.

Mississippian culture in Tuckaleechee Cove strongly resembled settlements at the time in other parts of eastern North America. Most of the houses found in excavations at the Big Dig were similar to Mississippian households of the upper Tennessee Valley peoples of the time (figure 33). Archaeologists refer to this culture as the Hiwassee Island phase, so named for a prehistoric town on an island where the Hiwassee River meets the Tennessee River in modern-day Meigs County, Tennessee. At the Hiwassee Island site, a palisade protected a central platform mound and several community buildings. Evident in every phase of the mound's use were two structures, each with a porch. These may have been the residence of the chief and his family and a place for official functions.[11]

The Hiwassee Island people and the Skittletown residents were involved in larger, more complex, and more widely spread social and political networks than the Woodland people had been. The greater complexity may have arisen from an increasing population that led to changes in leadership structure and organization, in which a hereditary chief and an elite class were responsible for organizing larger groups of people across a wider landscape.

An increasing food supply among the Mississippians enabled complex social organization. The expansion of foods resulted from the growing of corn, squash, and beans. Mesoamerican farmers from far to the south had first cultivated these crops. The people of Tuckaleechee Cove imported them and, for the first time in their history, began to grow more of their food than they collected from wild sources. Farming even changed their hunting practices because, instead of traveling to remote hunting grounds, their garden plots and agricultural fields became the "bait" for many animals. One can imagine that young hunters were responsible for protecting the crops from hungry animals. Deer, bear, turkey, various birds, and small mammals were all attracted to the fields. Archaeologists refer to this practice as garden hunting, and the bow and arrow was surely the decisive weapon in this activity.

---

11. Thomas M. N. Lewis and Madeline Kneberg, *Hiwassee Island: An Archaeological Account of Four Tennessee Indian Peoples* (Knoxville: University of Tennessee Press, 1946), is a classic in southeastern North American archaeology.

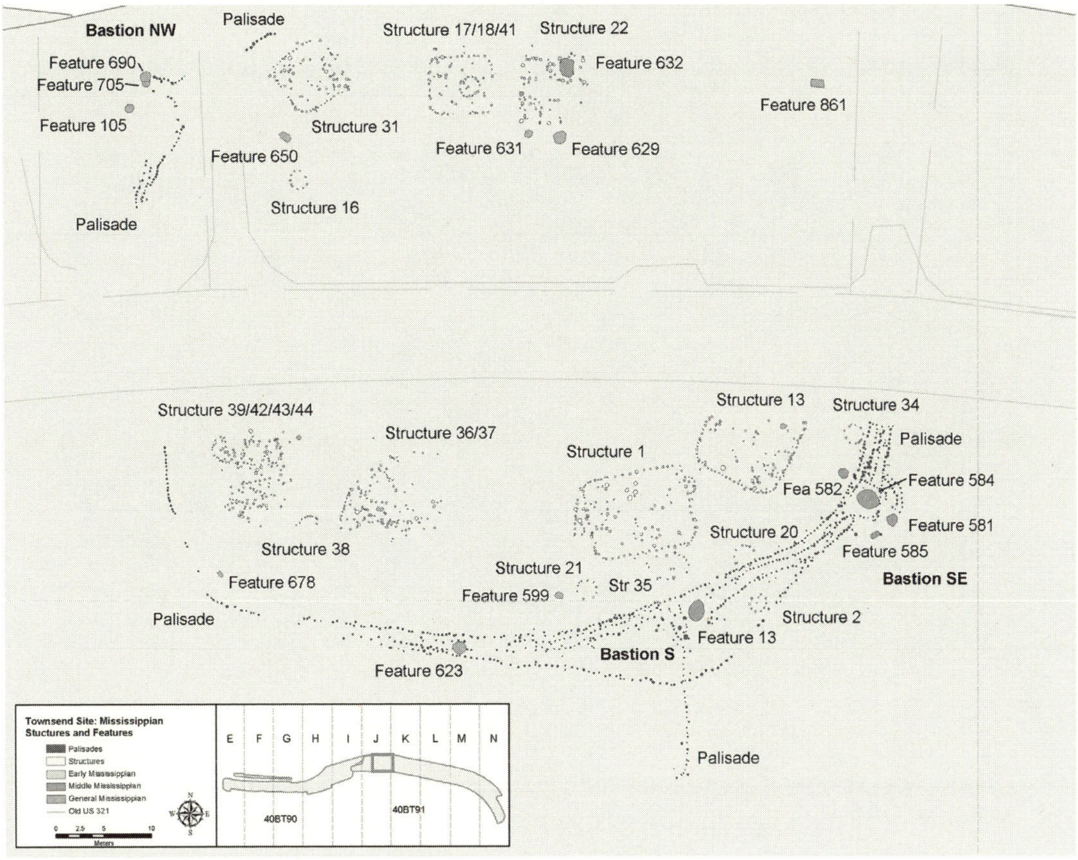

Figure 32. Schematic of Skittletown showing the location of palisades, buildings, and larger features.

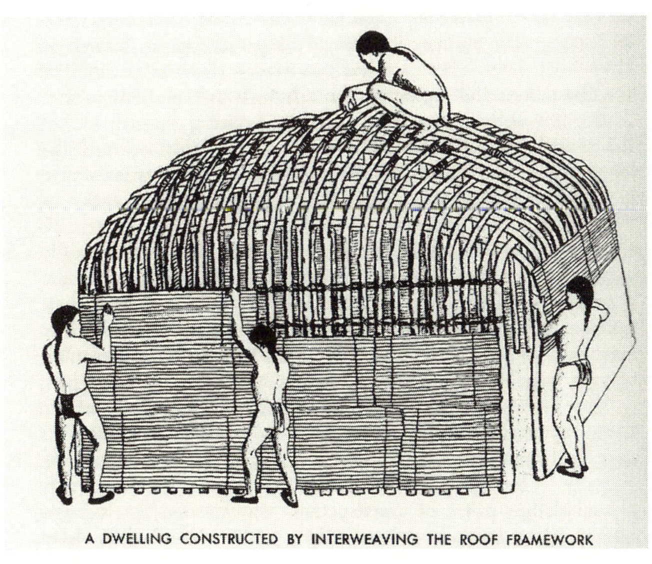

Figure 33. Houses similar to this artist's reconstruction of a Hiwassee Island house were found at Skittletown and the Mississippian farmsteads in Tuckaleechee Cove. (From Lewis and Kneberg, *Tribes That Slumber* [1958], 84.)

Figure 34. Post hole patterns of three corn cribs found during excavation at the Big Dig.

Intensive gardening of corn, beans, and squash and close protection of crops meant that food surpluses and storage became crucial issues. Archaeologists traced the change of storage facilities from the large pits of the Archaic people in the cove to smaller but more numerous storage pits of the Mississippians. Over a dozen sets of circular post patterns found at the Big Dig (figure 34) were interpreted as above-ground corn cribs for storage and protection of foodstuffs. Each structure consisted of a series of poles, anchored in a circular pattern in individual postholes, probably with an elevated platform, retaining walls, and a roof.

Who were the enemies of the Mississippian people? Archaeologists are certain that Skittletown and the cove in general were situated on the border between the Hiwassee Island culture to the west and mountain people to the east. Archaeologists have named the mountain culture of about 900 to 600 years ago the Pisgah phase of the Mississippian era. The Pisgah phase represents an Appalachian Summit culture that seems to be a unique development from as far back as Archaic times. Although influenced by Native American cultures in Georgia, the upper Tennessee Valley, and the Ohio Valley, the Pisgah phase retained distinctive traits including distinctive designs. Two Pisgah-phase houses were excavated at the Big Dig, although their dating from around 650 years ago may mean that these houses were occupied after the people of Skittletown had abandoned their village. Perhaps the Pisgah peoples shared the cove with people with ties to Hiwassee Island culture, or perhaps at this time, Pisgah people and those of the Hiwassee Island culture were contending for cove lands.[12]

In the lives of Mississippian people, there were two seasons—the cold season and the warm season. During the cold season, men were responsible for hunting and might be away from the village for an extended period on the hunt. Otherwise, warfare was a way a man could distinguish himself. Wars were organized on the principles of raiding and retaliation. A man strived to earn war names and battle honors to enhance his status as a warrior. Warriors retaliated for harm or death caused by another clan or another chiefdom. Raiding of another town was meant to terrorize it into submission. Many symbols found on Mississippian artifacts relate to warfare and to what archaeologists have called a warrior cult. The bow and arrow was the principal weapon, but the well-equipped warrior often carried a lance and war club.[13]

While men cleared the fields and built houses and palisades, women were responsible for all aspects of farming from planting until harvest. Thus, their larger responsibilities occurred in the warm season, although they worked year-round in collecting tasks and domestic activities. Women, or their lineage, probably owned the fields and the house. Men skinned animals from the hunt, but women prepared the skins and made garments and other articles from them. Children and the elderly assisted in the collecting, fishing, and trapping of small animals. Upon entering puberty, each person was initiated into his or her respective roles as an adult.

For the Mississippians, no part of life could be separated from their beliefs. Their belief system elaborated and embraced ideas about balance or order. To them, the world was composed of three levels. *This World*, the earth, was a flat island floating in a sea. Above it was the *Upper World*, a vault of the sky shaped like an overturned bowl that held up *This World* with four cords, each at a cardinal direction of north, south, east, and west. In the *Upper World* lived spiritual beings, including the Sun and Moon. The *Under World*, the area beneath the earth and including bodies of water, was also inhabited by spiritual beings. Water sources and caves were natural entrances to the Under World. Order and stability ruled in the Upper World, whereas the Under World was home to chaos and change. Elements of one world had to be kept separate from those of another world. These worlds controlled humans; there were no accidents or coincidences in life. People caused accidents when they mixed things from different worlds. For example, disaster resulted when water from the Under World was used to extinguish fire of This World.[14]

Religious ceremonies were intended to insure, or to restore, order in community life and purity to the individual. The open, central plaza of the Mississippian village was the site of these ceremonies. Chiefs led in the ritual practices because they were thought to be able to control some elements of their environment. Other ritual leaders were believed to have the gifts of foresight and curing. They carried small containers and tubes of herbal and magical cures used in rituals. The artifact pictured in figure 35 is sometimes called a "boatstone"

12. Roy S. Dickens, *Cherokee Prehistory: The Pisgah Phase in the Appalachian Summit Region* (Knoxville: University of Tennessee Press, 1976).

13. Hudson, *Southeastern Indians*, 225, 325–27.

14. For Mississippian culture, see Timothy Pauketat and Nancy Stone Bernard, *Cahokia Mounds* (New York: Oxford University Press, 2004); and Hudson, chapter 3, *The Southeastern Indians*.

Figure 35. Polished stone from the Townsend sites. The specimen may have been used in ritual curing, worn as a ornament or emblem (gorget) around the neck.

because of its shape. Excavated at the Big Dig, it might have held a magic potion, or it may have been part of a ritual leader's paraphernalia to administer cures. Alternatively, it might have served as a weight on an atlatl and in that role also held magic materials or a potion.

At this time, archaeologists can offer only plausible speculations. These speculations may be confirmed (or revised) later with new research techniques. If the past decades of archaeological research are any indication, presently unimagined techniques of analysis in the future will allow more informed conclusions.

Some artifacts found on Mississippian sites are images stamped into pottery vessels or cut into stone artifacts. These decorative elements may have reflected positions of high social status. Several artifacts were found decorated with animal designs. The stone pictured in plate 7 contained a lightly cut picture that appears to be a turtle. Another stone (figure 36) is shaped like a rattlesnake.

Mississippians took games seriously, especially young men whose reputation within the village and elsewhere depended on their abilities at gaming. The plaza at Skittletown was probably used for games such as "chunky." A highly polished disc, a chunky stone, was rolled through the plaza as contestants threw spears at the location where they thought the stone would stop. The contestant whose spear was closest to where the stone came to rest was the winner. Several stones of this shape were found in the remains at the Big Dig (figure 37 and plate 8). Competition was keen and often involved betting personal property. Mississippian villages competed against one another in chunky games, as well as in a popular stick

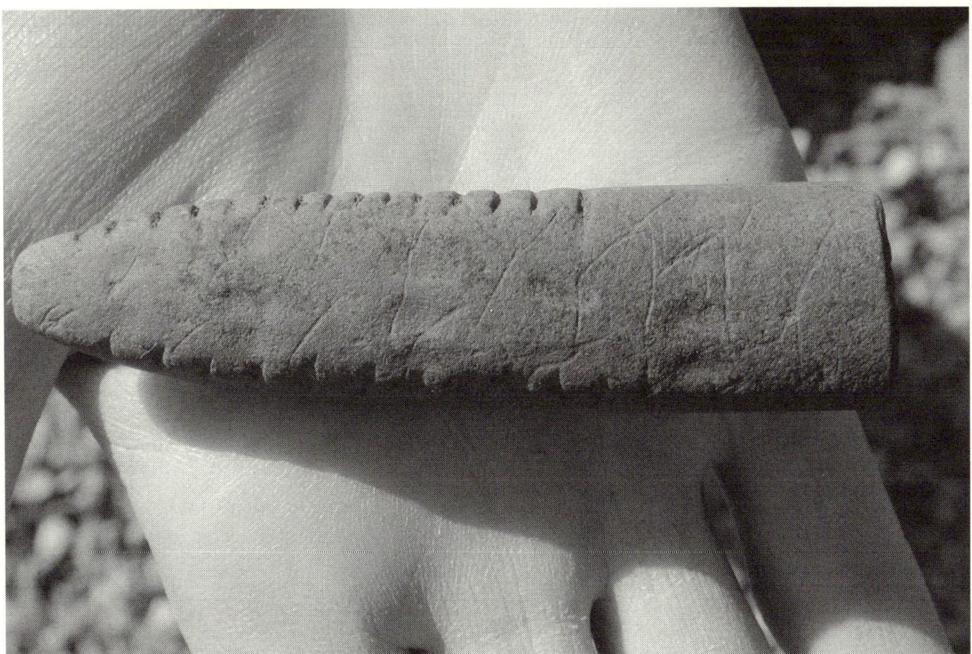

Figure 36. An incised design on this naturally shaped stone depicts the rattles on a snake.

Figure 37. Chunkey stone from the Big Dig. (See also plate 8.)

ball game, similar to lacrosse, in which dozens, even hundreds, of people played at one time. Mississippian towns often had a designated ball field with erect goal posts.

So, who were the people of Skittletown? Our best guess is that they were members of a chiefdom located in the Tennessee Valley some miles to the west. They probably lived and worked in Tuckaleechee Cove for a portion of each year, if not year-round, to raise crops and collect nuts in the old-fashioned way. Corncribs stored these surplus foodstuffs, and palisades and bastions protected them.

After Skittletown

What happened to the people in Tuckaleechee Cove after the demise of Skittletown about 650 years ago? Throughout eastern North America, chiefdoms rose and fell. They concentrated in major river valleys and created a borderland in peripheral areas used only for hunting and movement of warriors. Did Tuckaleechee Cove become one of these areas, seeing only the war and hunting parties as they traversed the mountains? Archaeologists do not really know, because few artifacts were left in the vicinity of the Big Dig during the period from 650 to 400 years ago. Archaeologists think some people occupied the cove during this period, but their cultural identity and their reasons for being there remain mysteries. Possibly in the future archaeologists will excavate new sites so that they can answer more questions.

The prehistoric period concluded with the arrival of explorers and then colonists from Europe. The history of Tuckaleechee Cove from five hundred to three hundred years ago is mostly in darkness, because no written records are known that might illuminate our story. Archaeologists and historians do know from other sources that interactions between Native Americans and explorers, traders, and colonists introduced new diseases for which Native Americans had no immunity. Large numbers of people died from epidemics, and the remnants of many communities were forced to relocate to other areas. Native populations were dislocated from the eastern coast of North America by European colonists. Such was the setting in the 1600s when our story begins a new chapter with the Cherokees of Tuckaleechee Cove.

Suggested Readings

Hudson, Charles. *The Southeastern Indians.* Knoxville: University of Tennessee Press, 1976. A very readable synthesis of research, writing, and eyewitness accounts by early explorers, traders, and trained ethnographic observers concerning aboriginal Southeastern peoples.

Lewis, Thomas M. N., and Madeline Kneberg. *Hiwassee Island: An Archaeological Account of Four Tennessee Indian Peoples.* Knoxville: University of Tennessee Press, 1946. Although this volume is a classic of the archaeological literature and somewhat dated, its limited use of archaeological jargon makes it quite accessible to a general audience. As such, this volume alone encapsulates much of our basic knowledge on the Mississippian period in the upper Tennessee Valley.

Sullivan, Lynne P., and Susan C. Prezzano, eds. *Archaeology of the Appalachian Highlands.* Knoxville: University of Tennessee Press, 2001. Although this volume of articles was written by archaeologists for the archaeological community, it can give the general reader considerable insight into the complexity of the prehistoric and historic Native American cultures of the Appalachian Mountains.

Chapter 3
THE CHEROKEES

Three centuries after Skittletown was built, several families of the Cherokee people made their homes along the bank of the Little River within the area of the Big Dig. Other Cherokee households undoubtedly existed in the cove. While archaeologists do not know the complete story of Cherokees within the cove, Cherokee remains found at the Big Dig came from the 1600s and early 1700s. The Big Dig found ten Cherokee homesteads featuring fire pits, hearths, postholes, and tools.[1]

Cherokee History and Geography

Cherokees populated the southern Appalachian landscape when EuroAmerican traders, soldiers, and explorers recorded their experiences with native residents. By 1700 they had documented that Cherokees lived in more than sixty communities. EuroAmericans divided the Cherokees into three divisions: Lower Settlements in present-day northwestern Georgia and northwestern South Carolina; the Middle and Valley Settlements in present-day North Carolina; and the Overhill Settlements—those west of the Appalachian crest—in present-day eastern Tennessee (figure 38). Differences in language and ceramic designs tell scholars that these divisions were accurate and that the differences were longstanding.

In the oldest historical documents, the Cherokees in the cove were referred to as the Tuckaleechee towns and were considered different from the Overhill towns of the Little Tennessee Valley. Based on households documented in the Big Dig, archaeologists now believe that Cherokee farmers living in the cove included households related to Cherokees east of the Appalachian summit while some were more closely related to the Overhill Cherokees of

1. Marcoux's *Pox, Empire, Shackles, and Hides* and his technical report *The Cherokees of Tuckaleechee Cove* detail the known Cherokee archaeological remains from Tuckaleechee Cove.

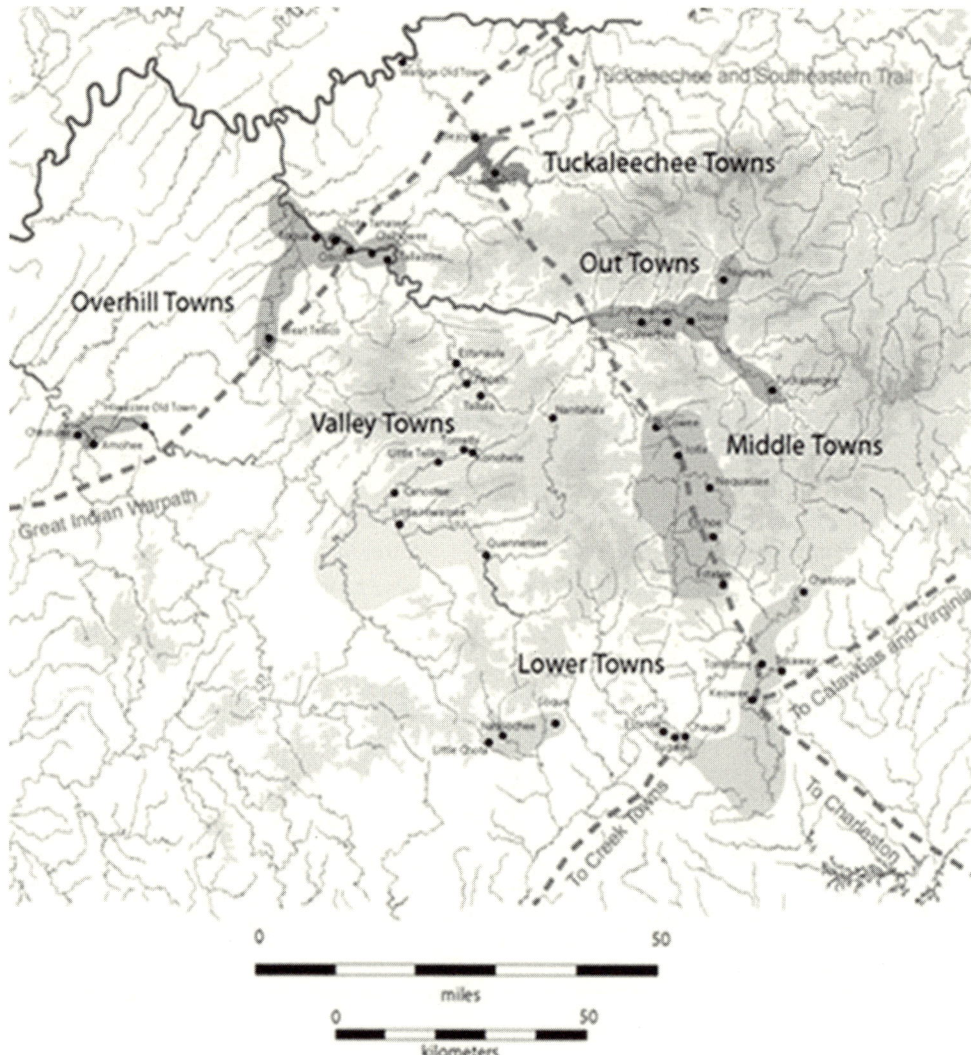

Figure 38. Cultural geography of Cherokee territory during the English Contact period, 1650 to 1715. (Map adapted by Marcoux 2010:55 from Duncan and Riggs, Cherokee Heritage Trails Guidebook [2003].)

the upper Tennessee Valley.[2] Jon Marcoux, an archaeologist who investigated the Cherokee remains from the Big Dig, referred to the Tuckaleechee Cherokees as a "coalescent community" composed of refugees from various areas of the Cherokee region.

A 1721 map called the area of the cove a "Deserted Settlement." The Cherokee town of Ellejoy, northwest of the cove at the confluence of Little River and Ellejoy Creek, was also

2. An early map, called the Barnwell-Hammerton map, of 1721 is depicted in plate 48 of William P Cumming, *The Southeast in Early Maps*, 3rd ed., rev. and enlarged by Louis De Vorsey Jr. (Chapel Hill: University of North Carolina Press, 1998). The map is also published as figure 4.2 in Marcoux, *Cherokees of Tuckaleechee Cove*, 28.

recorded on early maps but was reported in 1762 to have been long abandoned.[3] It seems likely that the Tuckaleechee towns were abandoned by the time of the Yamasee War in 1715, a huge conflict in which most native peoples in southeastern North America divided over whether to support or resist British encroachment. In the Yamasee War, the Cherokees chose to support the British while the Creek Indians from farther south resisted, placing the two Native American groups on opposing sides of the war.

Like their Mississippian predecessors, Cherokees placed their settlements on flat ground near streams and agricultural fields. Some Cherokee settlements could be considered towns by modern standards with closely spaced houses, but many settlements were collections of dispersed individual homesteads along waterways. Cherokee towns included both public buildings and domestic structures. During the building of the Tennessee Valley Authority's Tellico Reservoir about thirty miles west of Tuckaleechee Cove in the 1970s, several Cherokee towns were excavated. Most included up to sixty houses and civic structures used for public meetings in close proximity. These public buildings, of octagonal floor plan with benches lining the walls, often had large pavilions for warm-weather meetings. Cherokee settlements on the eastern side of the Appalachians had square townhouses but were otherwise organized in a similar way.[4]

Cherokee homesteads in the 1600s usually consisted of several building types. Unlike their Mississippian predecessors, who built rectangular houses, the Cherokee winter home was usually circular or sometimes octagonal. The homestead typically included both a winter and summer house. The winter house was enclosed, and the summer house an open rectangular structure, often with a gabled roof. The homestead usually included raised corncribs and various types of racks and benches. James Adair, an Irish-born trader, traveled among Cherokees during the early 1700s. He described their winter house as being built on "strong forked posts, at a proportional distance, in a circular form, all of an equal height, about five or six feet above the surface of the ground," on which they tied "large pieces of the heart of white oak." In the middle of the circle they sank four large pine posts in a quadrangle, and on top of them, they strapped heavy log rafters to which they attached "a number of long dry poles, all properly notched, to keep strong hold of the under posts and wall-plate." Then they wove between the roof rafters split saplings and daubed them "all over about six or seven inches thick with tough clay, well mixt with withered grass: when this cement is half dried, they thatch the house with the longest sort of dry grass."[5]

Of the ten areas within the Big Dig, six concentrations of Cherokee features and artifacts indicated reasonably complete patterns of Cherokee households. Two of the households

3. *The Memoirs of Lieutenant Henry Timberlake*, ed. S. C. Williams (1762; repr., Signal Mountain: Tennessee Mountain Press, 2001), 22–175.

4. Jefferson Chapman, *Tellico Archaeology: 12,000 Years of Native American History, 3rd. ed.* (Knoxville: University of Tennessee Press, 2014), provides a good description of Cherokee domestic and public architecture.

5. James Adair, *A History of the North American Indians* (1775; repr., New York: Promontory Press, 1986), 449–551. Adair, who lived and traded with Southeastern Indians, particularly the Chickasaws, between 1735 to 1768, is often quoted as an astute observer of Native American lifeways in the Southeast.

included both winter and summer structures, and one included a ramada, a lightweight structure for shade. Cherokee winter houses in Tuckaleechee Cove had hearths, as did some summerhouses. Some pits in the vicinity of houses provided storage, and raised corncribs like those at Skittletown may have been used. Probably for security, some storage was put inside houses. Homesteads seem to have been designed for nuclear families. No large Cherokee townhouses or public structures were identified at the Big Dig, although they were probably located outside the bounds of the excavations.

The most complete Cherokee homestead excavated during the Big Dig (figure 39) exhibited unusual characteristics in comparison to others. The homestead included a rectangular summerhouse that had forty-eight exterior posts and two larger posts set along its centerline, which must have supported a ridgepole for a gabled roof. Unlike some of the other summerhouses, this structure had closely spaced upright wall posts and two hearths. The winter house conformed to the typical architectural style for Cherokee houses with fifty-two upright posts forming an octagonal floor plan. It had four interior posts arranged in a square around a central hearth. Some posts supported interior benches. This winter house may have been covered with mud plaster (figure 40). Unlike other Cherokee households found at the Big

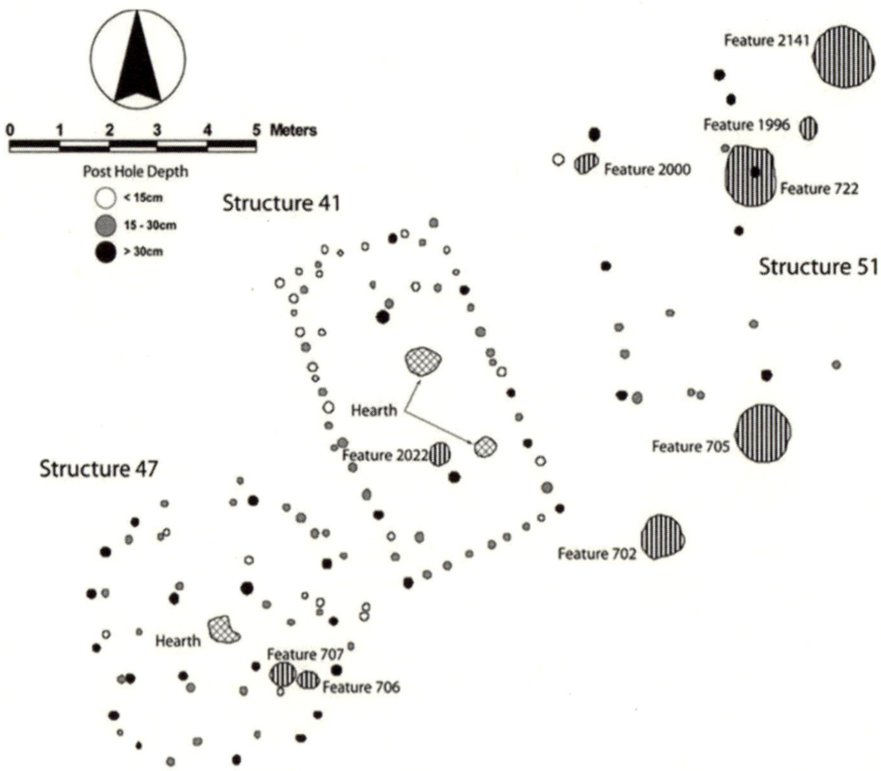

Figure 39. Cherokee household with summerhouse, winterhouse, and ramada excavated during the Big Dig.

Figure 40. *Top:* Excavation view of the Cherokee household shown in Figure 39. *Bottom:* A reconstructed image of a Cherokee homestead. (Drawing from *Schroedl, Overhill Cherokee Archaeology at Chota-Tanasee* [1986], 268.)

Dig, this household also had a ramada, which was rectangular with widely spaced exterior posts, no walls, and a shed-style roof. It was probably built to provide a shaded outdoor space for work and relaxing.

Six to eight individuals occupied each Cherokee household in Tuckaleechee Cove. Houses lasted for about eight to ten years, and there is little evidence that new houses were built on old household sites. To archaeologists, this means that the Cherokees of the cove lived under pressures to relocate homesteads on a frequent basis, but the nature of those pressures are not yet known. About 1800 the Cherokees adopted rectangular houses and log cabins, though by then they had long since abandoned the cove.

Cherokee Technology and Subsistence

Like the prehistoric Mississippians, Cherokee people tended crops of corn, beans, and squash and supplemented those with wild plants and game. The charred remains of plant parts, seeds, shells, and animal bone from Cherokee households excavated during the Big Dig indicate that they were fully engaged in corn agriculture. They grew the blue flowering plant now often called maypops or passionflower, but which the Cherokees called *ocoee* and for which the river in the southern Appalachians is named. They also tended little barley and other spinach-like plants (chenopod and goosefoot) as well as other species of edible and medicinal plants. Like their forebears, they collected hickory nuts, black walnuts, chestnuts, and acorns in season. They also gathered a wide variety of wild berries and grapes. The Cherokees were effective bow-and-arrow hunters of white-tailed deer and turkey, and they trapped rabbits, squirrels, and other small mammals. Their arrowheads differed slightly in style from earlier people, but like the Mississippians before them, they practiced garden hunting for fresh meat. They caught fish with hook and line, nets, and fish weirs, traps placed in streams to funnel fish into wicker baskets.[6]

Although metal tools were available to some Cherokees during the seventeenth century, this was not so for the Cherokees of Tuckaleechee Cove. They continued to employ chipped stone and ground-stone technology little different from their Mississippian and earlier forebears. Chipped stone technology relied on flaking stone to reduce and shape the mass. Most chipped stone tools were manufactured from chert, rocks with high silica content. Such rock was not available in Tuckaleechee Cove and probably came from downstream toward present-day Knoxville. Five similar types of triangular or oval arrow points made from chert were most popular among Cherokees of the cove (figure 41 and plate 17). In addition to making chipped stone tools, they shaped cobblestones found in the Little River and tributary creeks into hammer stones, anvils, nutting stones, and pestles. Cobblestones were also used as net sinkers for fishing. Hoe blades were roughly flaked from pieces of slate.

6. Kandace Hollenbach and her colleagues describe the subsistence remains, animal bone, and carbonized plant materials found in Cherokee artifacts at the Townsend sites in Marcoux, *Cherokees of Tuckaleechee Cove*, 179–206.

Figure 41. Three examples of chipped stone projectile points recovered from Cherokee contexts from the Big Dig.

Figure 42. Bowl of a Cherokee smoking pipe from the excavations at the Big Dig.

Finely ground stone artifacts included tomahawks and smoking pipes like the one pictured in figure 42. The Cherokee tool kit also included instruments made from chert to perforate, slice, and scrape various materials, including wood, bone, antler, and hide. Cherokee living sites were littered with chert and flint flakes, evidence that a sharp cutting tool was always close at hand. In Tuckaleechee Cove, Cherokees used stone tools, especially scrapers, for butchering and skinning animals and processing hides and leather.[7]

7. Jeremy Sweat conducted research on the origins of stone materials found at the Townsend sites and reported in his master's thesis, "Lithic Resource Survey of the Upper Little River Drainage." The stone tools found in Cherokee contexts at the Townsend sites are discussed by Boyce Driskell and colleagues in Marcoux, *Cherokees of Tuckaleechee Cove*, 137–56.

Some tools and weapons do not appear in the archaeological record because they were made of materials that were not preserved at the Big Dig. From written accounts by Euro-American observers, it is clear that Cherokees used the blowgun, made of a seven- to nine-foot length of cane, reamed out to provide a smooth bore for the projectile. The dart was about a foot long and usually carved from wood. It was sharply pointed and had several inches of animal hair lashed to its end to provide an air seal. These weapons, often used by boys, were deadly in expert hands for up to fifty feet in the hunt for birds and small animals.[8]

Archaeologists know that they can document only part of the rich material culture of the Cherokees. Many Cherokee technologies used perishable fiber. Mats, baskets, bags, and netting made of plant fibers were not preserved at the Big Dig but were surely used. Where the baskets have been found, they reveal a weaving technique in which the basket's fabric is fashioned by over-under movement of the fiber. A popular material was the outer portion of strips of river cane, often dyed in various colors. Cherokees made many varieties of baskets: small ones with handles, sieves for processing corn meal, large baskets for carrying big burdens, and baskets with tight-fitting covers. Artifacts of wood, such as fish traps, paddles, and handles for tools and weapons did not survive in the open environment of the Big Dig. Neither did the wooden images of animals, humans, and mystical beings that the Cherokees typically carved into masks.[9]

The material culture of the Cherokees uncovered at the Big Dig was nearly all of traditional manufacture, although contact and exchange with EuroAmericans influenced the Cherokees in other, less remote areas. They replaced stone tools with iron implements they acquired from white traders, although only one small piece of iron was found in a Cherokee context at the Big Dig. Cherokees adopted some European plants, including peaches and black-eyed peas, and raised European-imported animals, especially pigs, but these domesticates were not found at the Big Dig. Traditional pottery was more resistant to European influence; ceramic wares and styles persisted into the time of EuroAmerican contact. The best evidence of EuroAmerican contact with Cherokees from Tuckaleechee Cove came from 228 glass beads made in Europe (figure 43 and plate 18). Based on a comparative analysis of changes in glass beads through time, the ones recovered during the Big Dig probably date from 1650 to 1720.[10]

Cherokee artifacts found on opposite sides of the Appalachian Mountains differed from each other. To the east, Cherokee communities produced ceramics in an ancient, unbroken tradition of manufacture that archaeologists can trace over the course of about five hundred years. Referred to as the Qualla ceramics series, the eastern ceramic jars and bowls were

8. Hudson, *The Southeastern Indians*, 272–89, presents an extensive discussion on weapons and hunting in southeastern Native American cultures, including the Cherokees.

9. Ibid., 376–85. See also Sarah H. Hill, *Weaving New Worlds: Southeastern Cherokee Women and their Basketry* (Chapel Hill: University of North Carolina Press, 1997).

10. Marcoux, *Cherokees of Tuckaleechee Cove*, 157–78.

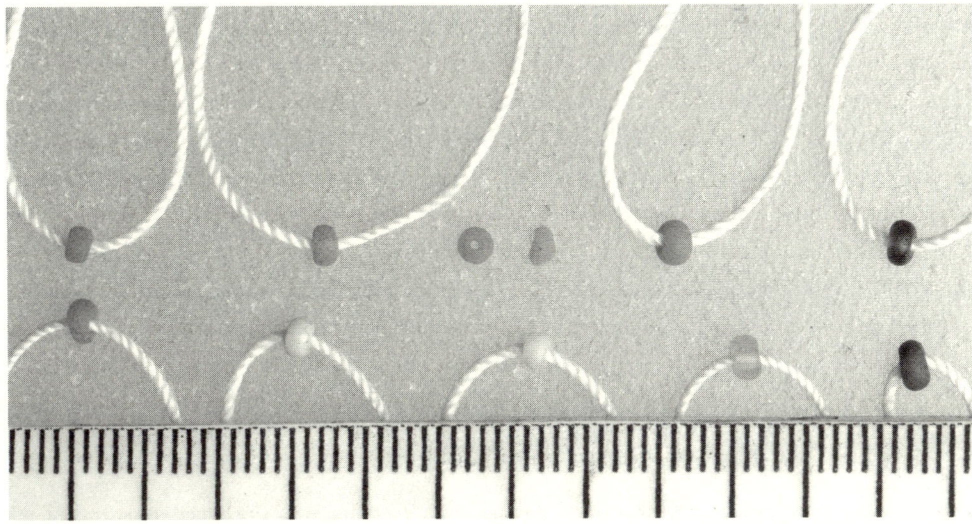

Figure 43. Glass trade beads like this sample from the Big Dig (scale is in millimeters) were used to establish dates for each Cherokee household.

marked with curved and rectangular designs cut into the clay and impressions made by fingers in the clay rims. Designs were applied either by pressing wooden paddles with cut patterns into damp clay or by cutting the ceramic clay with a sharp-edged piece of flint. On the west side of the mountains, Overhill ceramics were similar to Mississippian ceramics, tempered with burned, ground shells. Some Overhill Cherokee ceramic vessels were decorated by stamping in a checked design, and some bore corncob markings or designs made when a stick wrapped with cord was rolled along the surface of damp clay. Overhill ceramics included various sizes of bowls, globe-shaped jars, and flat-bottomed pans.[11]

However, Cherokee households in Tuckaleechee Cove showed three separate ceramic styles. Two households had ceramics that looked like Overhill pots. These households, probably Overhill descendants who had settled in Tuckaleechee Towns, were most likely longtime residents in the cove. Pottery from another house looked more like the traditional Qualla wares from east of the mountains. The members of that household were probably

11. Qualla ceramics define the Qualla phase, a period spanning late prehistoric into historic times. For more information, see Bennie Keel, *Cherokee Archaeology: A Study of the Appalachian Summit* (Knoxville: University of Tennessee Press, 1976), 40–45, 214–16; Overhill Cherokee ceramics are different from Qualla ceramics and seem to derive from earlier types present in the Upper Tennessee valley as late as 1600 A.D. Many of these vessels are without decoration. These ceramics are related to the Mississippian tradition that preceded the Overhill Cherokees and that spread in late prehistoric times from the Mississippi River Basin eastward along major waterways. See Gerald Schroedl's brief description of Chota-Tanasee in Gibbon, *Archaeology of Prehistoric Native America*, 150–52.

recent migrants to the cove. But three households produced pots tempered with small pieces of gravel and decorated with paddle stamping. This mixture of techniques and decorative motifs from both sides of the mountains is so far unique to Cherokee households found at the Big Dig and has been named "Tuckaleechee Wares." This mixture might reflect the work of people with longer tenure in the cove. Several generations would be required for potters to adopt and meld techniques from each longstanding ceramic tradition.

The differences of pottery among households in the cove suggest a historical pattern for Cherokees in the cove: an archaeologist has suggested that they were a collection of displaced people from other areas. In other words, new faces were constantly entering the cove from at least the 1600s.[12]

Cherokee Social Structure and Ethnicity

The Cherokee belief system resembled that of their Mississippian predecessors and other Native American groups living in southeastern North America in the 1600s and 1700s. The Cherokee language is a member of the Iroquoian languages and the most southern of those languages whose other members are historically based far to the north near the Great Lakes. As with the Mississippian peoples, family descent and residence were determined by the mother. Social standing was based almost exclusively on clan, lineage, and personal ability and achievement. A household was composed of a nuclear family that maintained close ties with, and probably lived in close proximity to, members of their local lineage. The most important affiliation for a Cherokee person was the clan. Cherokees were organized into seven clans that did not allow marriage between two people of the same clan.

Unlike earlier Mississippians or many other contemporary Native American groups in the Southeast, Cherokee society lacked an upper class or nobles. This was a source of confusion and frustration for EuroAmerican administrators. They wanted to deal with a single individual who could speak for all Cherokees, much as the king ruled all of England. But because of their cultural traditions of social and political organization, this concept made no sense to the Cherokees.

Cherokee villages preferred independence and often acted in self-interest rather than for the benefit of all Cherokees everywhere. They upheld a long political tradition of local autonomy and divisions along generational and regional lines.

Little evidence was found from excavations during the Big Dig about the effects of the European diseases, the trade in Indian slaves, or the geographical displacement that devastated the Native American population between 1500 and 1800. But Cherokees elsewhere were certainly affected by those events and pressures. Most deadly to Native Americans were the smallpox and measles that Europeans carried. One estimate is that by 1700 the pre-European-contact population of about 30,000 Cherokees was reduced to 10,000 individuals.

12. Marcoux, *The Cherokees of Tuckaleechee Cove*, 105–36.

One of the largest effects of contact with Europeans was the overhunting of deer to supply traders with deerskins, which Native Americans traded for guns. A Cherokee hunter could earn up to $1,600 from EuroAmerican traders for the deerskins collected during a successful hunting season. The Cherokees certainly felt the shattering impact of European contact, but archaeological investigation has suggested that those in Tuckaleechee Cove did not experience directly the effects of European invasion. The cove may have become a haven for displaced people from other areas. The three pottery traditions in the Cherokee households in Tuckaleechee Cove support this theory.[13]

During the British colonial period in North America, from 1607 to 1776, most Cherokees were little known to EuroAmericans and to recorded history. They preferred to stay hidden in their mountainous homeland and to try to withstand the effects of rampant disease and the British demands for deerskins. But in 1715 when the Cherokees entered the Yamasee War on the side of English colonists and fought the Creeks, their isolation was broken. Needing firearms to fight the war, the Cherokees escalated their participation in deerskin trade. The archaeological evidence of Cherokee life in the cove stops at about 1720, but historical documents suggest that some Cherokees still occupied the Tuckaleechee Towns in 1740. Cherokees may have abandoned the area later in the 1740s as a result of a smallpox epidemic that ravaged the region. After that time, nearly all the individuals in Tuckaleechee Cove who appear in historical documents were of EuroAmerican origin.

Suggested Readings

Cockran, David H. *Cherokee Frontier: Conflict and Survival, 1740–62*. Norman: University of Oklahoma Press, 1962.

———. *The Eastern Band of Cherokees, 1819–1900*. Knoxville: University of Tennessee Press, 1984. This volume traces the early history of the EBCI, the group of Cherokees that remained in North Carolina after removal.

Marcoux, Jon Bernard. *Pox, Empire, Shackles, and Hides: The Townsend Site, 1670–1715*. Tuscaloosa: University of Alabama Press, 2010. This book summarizes Marcoux's dissertation research on the Cherokee households found at the Big Dig.

Mooney, James. *Myths of the Cherokee: Nineteenth Annual Report of the Bureau of American Ethnology*. Washington, DC: Smithsonian Institution, 1900. Although less available to the general public, this publication is an authoritative description of Cherokee myths.

13. See Marcoux, *Pox, Empire, Shackles, and Hides*; and John Haywood, *The Civil and Political History of the State of Tennessee from Its Earliest Settlement up to the Year 1796, Including the Boundaries of the State* (Knoxville, TN: Heiskell and Brown, 1823), 39.

Chapter 4
EUROAMERICANS IN THE COVE

Archaeologists and historians agree that few human beings showed their faces in Tuckaleechee Cove in the mid-1700s. Most of the Cherokees had left or died. The EuroAmericans did not arrive until near the end of the 1700s. One can imagine that the Cherokee homesteads built in the 1600s fell into ruin, and the gardens and crop fields returned to dense natural vegetation. One observer who saw Tuckaleechee Cove during that time was Henry Timberlake, a British colonial militia officer assigned to the Cherokees as a military attaché. Between 1756 and 1765, Timberlake traveled in eastern Tennessee and for a short time camped along the Little River. Timberlake testified to the Cherokee abandonment of the area, and he wondered how the natives could leave "so beautiful and fertile a spot." He thought that if the cove were closer to other settlements, "it would make the finest situation for a gentleman's seat I ever saw."[1]

The first EuroAmericans to visit Tuckaleechee Cove were traders. Far beyond the bustling coastal towns of colonial North America, even past the fall lines of every river that emptied into the Atlantic Ocean, a trader known to the historical record only as Vaughn left the relative safety of his Shenandoah Valley home in 1740 and began a trip that took him deep into Cherokee country. In the hope of exchanging goods, Vaughn made his way down the valley, crossed the New and Holston Rivers, passed by present-day Rogersville, and paddled along the French Broad before following well-worn Indian trails beside the Little River to the Tuckaleechee Towns. Although two Irish traders, Alexander Dougherty and James Adair, had earlier traveled extensively among the Cherokees, Vaughn became the earliest trader to record his visit to the cove. He did not leave details of what he saw there, and there is no archaeological record of his visit. After a short stay, he returned to Virginia but visited Tuckaleechee at other times until the outbreak of the French and Indian War in

1. *The Memoirs of Lieutenant Henry Timberlake*, ed. S. C. Williams (1762; repr., Signal Mountain: Tennessee Mountain Press, 2001), 22–175.

1754 made the journey too dangerous. Years of fighting among the French and English and their Indian allies disrupted primitive trade routes, and Vaughn never returned to the cove.[2]

For traders like Vaughn to move safely in eastern Tennessee, they had to maintain good relationships with local Indians. They became interpreters and unofficial diplomats between colonial governments and Native American tribes, with whom they oversaw trade agreements and political treaties. In the process, the two groups created a fluid but delicate middle ground in which neither culture dominated nor was in full control. Before the French and Indian War, colonial governments attempted to stymie western settlement by creating new laws restricting colonists from the backcountry. In North Carolina the royal governor closed western land that included Tuckaleechee Cove to new settlement in hopes of preserving the fragile balance of power on the frontier. But a few settlers simply ignored the governor's orders and continued their search for land until the political turmoil of the 1750s and 1760s made it too risky, though apparently none made it to the cove.[3]

After the conclusion of the French and Indian War in 1763, the British government tried to enforce bans on western settlement to avoid hostilities with Indians. It drew a line along the length of the Appalachian Mountains and issued the Proclamation of 1763 that established the Southern Indian Boundary Line as the official western boundary for British America. But the proclamation did little to halt western migration. Settlers continued to move over the Appalachians and to settle on the western slopes. In hopes of regaining control of its western boundary, the British appointed a superintendent of the Southern District for Indian Affairs to manage western land distribution and commercial trade, but that did not stop animosity on the frontier. Between 1763 and 1775, British officials failed to stop the westward migration of colonial settlers, and in 1768 they rescinded the Proclamation of 1763.[4]

The Tyranny of the Treaties

As settlers trickled into the Great Smoky Mountains, anxieties grew among EuroAmerican settlers and the Cherokees. Only an uneasy balance existed between the two groups. Neither

2. The best works for understanding the early contact between EuroAmerican traders and the Tuckaleechee Cove and Blount County areas are Haywood, *The Civil and Political History of the State of Tennessee*, 40–41; Inez E. Burns, *History of Blount County, Tennessee: From War Trail to Landing Strip, 1795–1957* (Nashville: Tennessee Historical Commission, 1957), 44; Paul Fink, "Early Explorers in the Great Smokies," *East Tennessee Historical Society's Publications* 5 (1933): 56.

3. Two recent scholarly works that analyze the process of EuroAmerican exploration and the emerging pattern of relations between them and the Native Americans are James H. Merrell, *Into the American Woods: Negotiators on the Pennsylvania Frontier* (New York: W. W. Norton, 1999), 26–27; and Richard White, *The Middle Ground: Indians, Empires, and the Republics in the Great Lakes Region, 1650–1815* (New York: Cambridge University Press, 1991), x–xiii. Older works with specific details on East Tennessee are Verner W. Crane, *The Southern Frontier, 1670–1732* (Tuscaloosa: University of Alabama Press, 1929), 154–55; and Alberta and Carson Brewer, *Valley So Wild: A Folk History* (Knoxville: East Tennessee Historical Society, 1975), 41.

4. Clarence E. Carter, "British Policy towards the American Indians in the South, 1763–8," *English Historical Review* 33 (1918): 39–41; Louis De Vorsey Jr., *The Indian Boundary in the Southern Colonies, 1763–1775* (Chapel Hill: University of North Carolina Press, 1961) 97–102.

side had the military power or economic strength to dominate the other. After the American Revolution reshaped the political landscape, new attempts to regain control of the frontier emerged. In 1783 North Carolina land speculators prematurely claimed more than 4 million acres of western land. Appalled by this blatant act of greed, citizens petitioned for the land to become part of the new state they named Franklin. The movement eventually faltered but not before John Sevier, the acting territorial governor, signed the Treaty of Dumplin Creek in 1785. The treaty opened Cherokee land south of the French Broad River in present-day Knox, Sevier, and Blount Counties to white settlement. A small group of Cherokees signed the treaty, apparently without authority. Old Tassel, a member of the Cherokee delegation, declared that several young men "had no authority to treat about lands." But after the treaty was signed, whites appointed their own men to settle land disputes and took the land. "We hope you, our elder brother, will not agree to it, but will have them moved off," Old Tassel pleaded. Later events showed that Indian land, once given up, if only by an unauthorized minority of Cherokees, was never recovered.[5]

In 1791 Governor William Blount of the Southwest Territory signed the Treaty of Holston to try to reconcile the Cherokees to white settlers by demarcating Indian land. Like the Treaty of Dumplin Creek, the Treaty of Holston resolved few disputes and did little to ease tensions. It promised Cherokees much land in eastern Tennessee, and Blount also agreed to pay an annual fee to the Cherokees. But in 1792 surveyors employed by the United States, including Charles McClung, established a boundary line that took away all Cherokee land south of the Tennessee River, including Tuckaleechee Cove. During this time, McClung and James Lackey were acquiring tens of thousands of acres of Tennessee land on which they speculated, including large tracts along the Little River in Tuckaleechee Cove. In 1792 Governor Blount sent a letter to the United States War Department saying that "no settlements can be formed" in the area that included Cades Cove, Tuckaleechee Cove, Wears Cove, and Millers Cove and other bottomlands. By 1794 conditions had deteriorated to the point that whites demanded forts for protection, including one in Tuckaleechee Cove that was not built.

After Tennessee achieved statehood in June 1796, Drury Paine Armstrong, a prominent Knoxvillian, registered many land claims with the state. Armstrong used the names of family members to claim land from the government, and then he had the land titles transferred to his own name. In this way he obtained 50,000 acres along the Little River. He and his heirs subsequently made a fortune selling or renting this land to settlers.[6]

In 1797 Benjamin Hawkins, the general superintendent of Indian Affairs for the United States, ordered another boundary line, and his surveyors reaffirmed Cherokee rights to

5. Mary U. Rothrock, "Carolina Traders among the Overhill Cherokees, 1690–1790," *East Tennessee Historical Society's Publications* 1 (1929): 14–17; John P. Brown, *Old Frontiers: The Story of the Cherokee Indians from Earliest Times to the Date of Their Removal to the West, 1838* (Kingsport, TN: Southern Publishers, 1938), 243–44.

6. Margaret L. Brown, *The Wild East: A Biography of the Great Smoky Mountains* (Gainesville: University Press of Florida, 2000), 7.

lands that included Tuckaleechee Cove. Hawkins's surveyors found two white "intruders" in Tuckaleechee Cove. One of them was probably John White, who in 1795 had been granted a right by the just-created Blount County Court, based in nearby Maryville, to build a public mill. It is clear from this that the national policies set by Hawkins and those made by local government in Tennessee were at odds.

Unable to keep settlers off their land, the Cherokees hoped to hold on to some land by reaffirming their friendship with white settlers. In 1798 EuroAmericans and Cherokees signed the First Treaty of Tellico, which redrew new settlement boundaries again. The treaty was intended to protect some lands for Indians, but it also opened most of Blount County to settlement. It also attempted to prevent future misunderstandings by appointing a treaty commission of representatives from the United States and the Cherokee Nation. The Tellico Treaty of 1798 eased settler fears, and people left Greene County, North Carolina, crossed the mountains into Cove Creek and Wears Cove, and followed the Little River to Tuckaleechee Cove. Other settlers followed the old paths from upper East Tennessee along the Little River into the cove. Rich river-bottom land, accessible by land and water, enticed settlers. Blount County work crews began marking and grading a new road from Maryville to Tuckaleechee Cove.[7]

All the treaties, it seemed, failed to protect the Cherokees from settler encroachment on their land. In 1806 the State of Tennessee formally recognized the rights of white occupants to stay where they were on lands of disputed control, like those in Tuckaleechee Cove. At the same time, when the United States Congress settled a boundary dispute between Tennessee and North Carolina over lands in the area of the Great Smoky Mountains, it recognized squatter's rights. Under the terms of Calhoun's Treaty in 1819, all remaining Cherokee claims to land south of Tuckaleechee Cove were forfeited. The treaty did not force out any Cherokees, but it did grant land to whites who already had settled there. In actuality, it was the final displacement of Cherokees from that region of the country.[8]

The Foundation of a New Community in Tuckaleechee Cove, 1800–1840

Tuckaleechee Cove emerged from the chaos of the 1700s to become a peaceful and prosperous EuroAmerican community in the 1800s. Settlers built homes, cleared and cultivated land, and raised families. Although it seemed isolated from nearby communities, Tuckaleechee Cove was in fact a part of an ever-widening web of East Tennessee towns and small cities with larger regional ties to the world beyond. Early roads connected it to larger markets. Roads also linked Tuckaleechee Cove to more remote mountain areas like Cades Cove. By

7. Burns, *History of Blount County*, 32.

8. Ibid., 271; Charles J. Kappler, *Indian Affairs: Laws and Treaties*, vol. 2 (Washington, DC: U.S. Government Printing Office, 1904), 29–33, 52–53; Mary U. Rothrock, *The French Broad–Holston Country: A History of Knox County, Tennessee* (Knoxville: East Tennessee Historical Society, 1946), 42–44.

1832 mail went twice a week from Tuckaleechee Cove to Maryville and Sevierville. Before any of this could happen, however, early settlers had to establish themselves on the frontier in Tuckaleechee Cove.

White settlement increased quickly after the signing of the last treaties. In an effort to thwart the tendency of land speculators like Charles McClung and Drury Armstrong, the State of Tennessee granted land directly to twelve men in Tuckaleechee Cove in 1807. The grants ranged from one of 34 acres to Samuel Rowland to one of 268 acres to William Davidson. Several of the twelve grants were quickly sold to others. Those who stayed in Tuckaleechee Cove settled side by side on both sides of the Little River. Like the prehistoric farmers who preceded them, they wanted access to water and the richest soils of the bottomland along Little River. Their settlement patterns were based on the same decisions that the Mississippians and Cherokees had made—that proximity to the river provided transportation connections and good farmland. They typically acquired as much adjacent land as they could buy (see figure 44 for a map of early land grants in Tuckaleechee Cove).

Despite the steady increase in settlement in the cove in the early 1800s, families came and went. Several settlers left in about 1815, for reasons unknown, but around the same time a group of families arrived from Greene County, Tennessee. This rapid turnover of population was typical of communities throughout the United States in the 1800s. Soon clusters of settlement formed up and down the cove. Each location had a name, and often it was a colorful one. Frog Town, Sunshine, Nogger's Knob, Kinzel Springs, and Needmore soon were place names in the cove. In time stores and mills were built to serve the needs of the families clustered in a place.

Most early families in Tuckaleechee Cove relied heavily on the abundance of trees to build homes, barns, and outbuildings. Most early residents built one-and-a-half-story cabins with one large room and a few windows. They cut and dragged nearby trees to a building site and then bound the logs together with a variety of notches. The saddle notch, full-V notch, half-dovetail notch, and the square notch were most popular in East Tennessee. Although poplar and oak were abundant in the area, many Blount County residents preferred pine for home building. After filling the gaps between logs with mud and constructing a roof, most builders added a fireplace, a floor, windows, and doors to their new homes.[9]

Tuckaleechee Cove families were mostly self-reliant out of necessity, but they also depended on manufactured products and outside services. Rural residents bought European manufactured goods as well as products made in nearby Maryville and Knoxville. Peter Snider established the first store in the cove. Rural farmers shipped corn, wheat, and timber to mills in Tuckaleechee Cove and either used or sold what they produced.

9. The best sources on EuroAmerican house architecture in Tuckaleechee Cove are John T. Morgan, "The Decline of Log House Construction in Blount County, Tennessee" (PhD diss., Dept. of Geography, University of Tennessee, 1986), 44–47, 61, 108–112; and Ed Trout, *Historic Buildings of the Smokies* (Gatlinburg, TN: Great Smoky Mountains Natural History Association, 1995), 20–26.

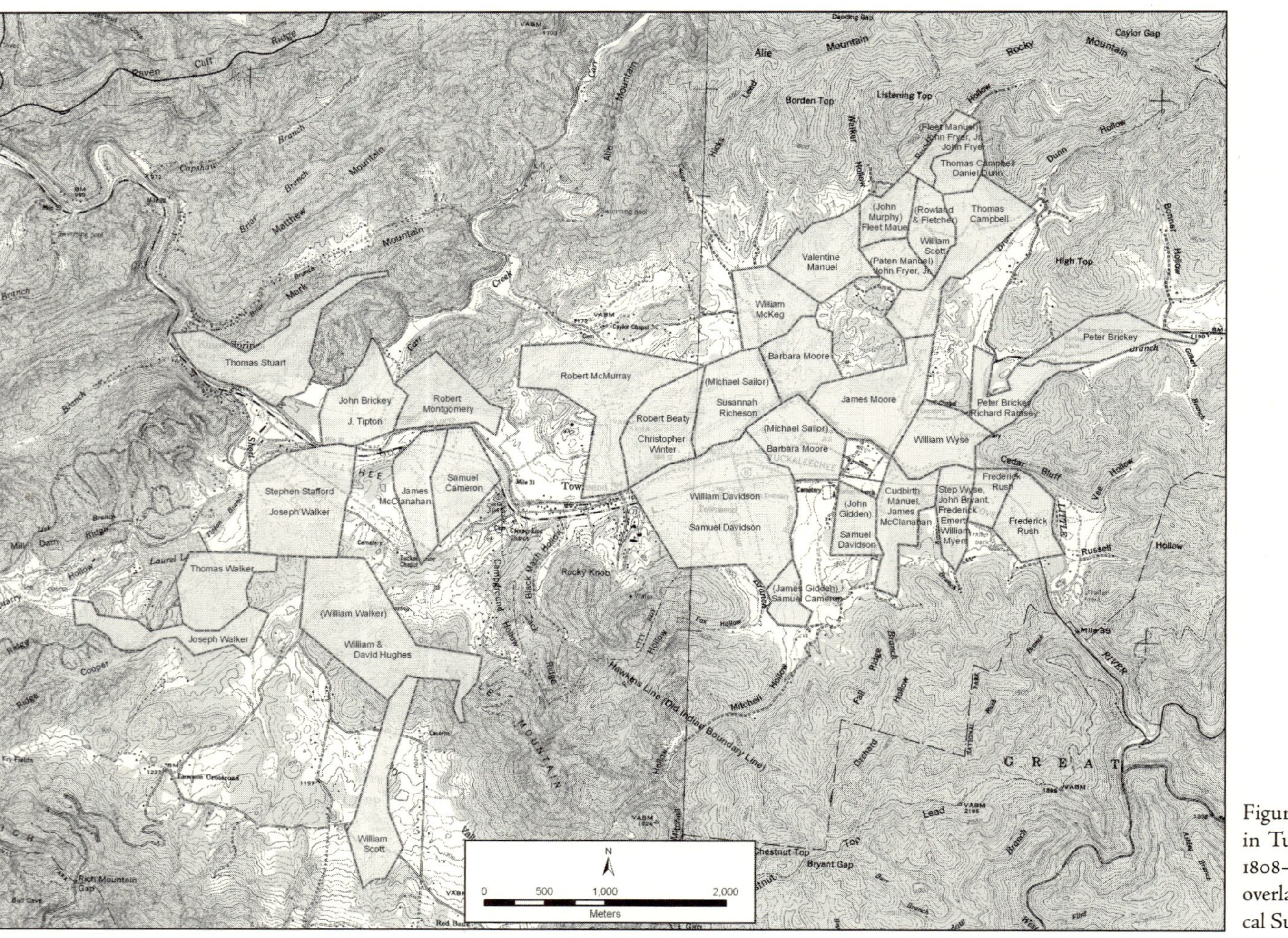

Figure 44. Land grants in Tuckaleechee Cove, 1808–14. (Staff drawing overlaid on US Geological Survey maps.)

The Archaeological Record for Life in Tuckaleechee Cove in the 1800s

The Big Dig excavated the sites of EuroAmerican homesteads, just as it had uncovered various Native American home sites. One important homestead was that of the Emert family, who ran a general store in Tuckaleechee Cove. Frederick Emert, born in 1754 in Pennsylvania, migrated to Sevier County and then to Tuckaleechee Cove with his wife and children in 1826. They probably lived somewhere else in the cove before they arrived at the place that would become their permanent home, which was excavated. They settled on previously owned property on which there was a log cabin. Several generations of Emerts lived there after Frederick died.[10]

Archaeologists excavated the Emert farmstead (figure 45), which included a cellar (figure 46), trash deposits or "middens," a well (figure 47), and a barn site. They found forty-nine artifacts they could identify, including horseshoes, nails, various iron tools, glass, and many pieces of various kinds of ceramics, most of which dated from the late 1800s. This archaeological record suggests that food-storage containers changed from crocks and jugs in the early 1800s to patterned glassware later in the century. Most of the ceramics were plain, white plates and cups, but there were some decorative pieces like colorful teapots. Among the artifacts were patent-medicine bottles that originated in places as nearby as Knoxville and others that apparently came from much farther away.

Excavation of the Emert farmstead and others nearby reveal an important reality about life in the cove after white settlement. It tells us that even though people seemed geographically

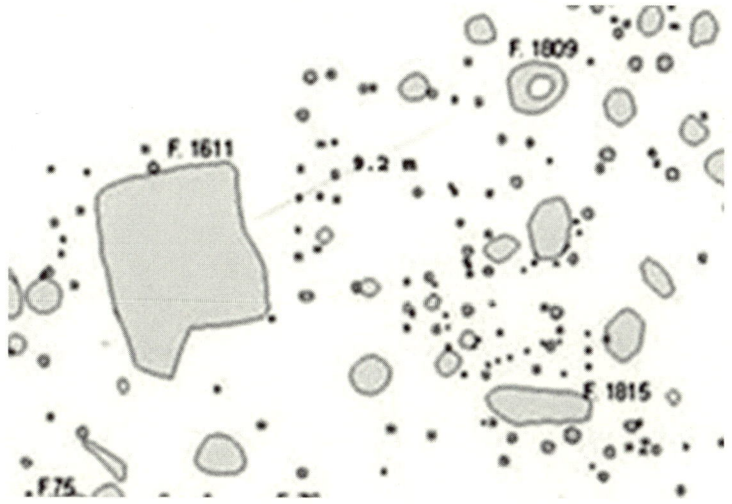

Figure 45. Excavation map of the Emert Farm showing the cellar (F. 1611) and hand dug well (F. 1809).

10. Burns, *History of Blount County*, 54.

Figure 46. Partially excavated cellar on the Emert Farm. Rocks result from filling of cellar after it was abandoned.

Figure 47. View of the river-cobble-lined, hand-dug well at the Emert Farm.

isolated there, and that they produced most of what that consumed, residents still used the things, the consumer goods, used by people living in urban places. This was more true for the second half of the 1800s, but commercial centers and means of transportation were sufficiently well established for the first white settlers of Tuckaleechee Cove to have an interesting mixture of household goods. (plate 19) Some were made nearby, but others were manufactured far away. This meant that they had some access to advertising, enjoyed transportation sufficient to have the goods delivered safely, and could rely on mercantile businesses to procure the desired items. The archaeological record from the Big Dig during the first century of EuroAmerican settlement testifies not only to settlers' self-sufficiency but also to their desire and ability to buy things from the outside world.

Archaeologists also excavated remnants of another farm, the Cameron farm, during the Big Dig. An interesting source of information pertaining to this farm is an oil painting of the farmhouse and associated outbuildings (figure 48). The painting shows a one-and-one-half-story sided house with a small one-story rear addition on the west end and a stone chimney. A barn and smaller outbuilding are a short distance to the west and south of the house. When the Little River Railroad was constructed, the tracks came fairly close to the house so it was reportedly moved to the south to be farther from the tracks.

The Importance of Early Mills

Water-powered mills on the Little River played an important economic role in Tuckaleechee Cove. They represented progress and profit for the community and for individual millers.

Figure 48. Painting of the James and Martha Cameron house. (Photograph courtesy of Les Rines.)

Mills became the center of economic and social activity. They ground corn and wheat and sawed lumber for both local residents and for markets beyond the cove. Early milling attempts in the cove failed until John Chambers opened one in the early 1800s. His mill succeeded and became a gathering point in a community isolated by wilderness and hampered by poor roads. Traveling merchants often congregated at mills during harvest time to do business. Blacksmiths and coopers opened shops near mills. Entire families rode to the mill to visit with friends and family as the miller ground their harvest.[11]

Millwrights like Chambers had to find a suitable site with adequate nearby waterpower. They had to take into consideration river conditions and the steepness of the riverbank when choosing a mill site and design. Early millers chose from three wheel designs. The tub, undershot, and overshot wheels (figure 49) offered millers a variety of benefits and drawbacks. Early millers in the Tuckaleechee area used the tub wheel as an easy option on shallow streams. Although simple to build and operate, the tub wheel required heavy maintenance because it lay horizontal in the middle of a stream. The vertical undershot wheel required a millrace to direct water against the bottom of the wheel. This wheel allowed millers to build along wider, gentler sections of a river or stream, which decreased the chances of flood damage. The overshot wheel became the most popular design in many rural areas. Although expensive to build and operate, the overshot mill generated more power and could complete jobs more quickly. It became a highly popular machine in nineteenth-century manufacturing.[12]

After constructing the mill house and wheel, millwrights in Tuckaleechee Cove installed wooden gears to transfer the vertical power of the waterwheel to the horizontal actions of millstones. Gearing converted the slow rotation of the waterwheel into over two hundred rotations per minute on a set of good millstones. At these speeds, any spark from the heavy millstones might ignite dust in the air. Millstones, either custom made by local wheelwrights or imported from France or Germany, were precious tools. Produced in matching pairs, these stones weighed several hundred pounds apiece and had to be installed with great care. The farmer and miller weighed the corn or wheat, or measured the timber, and from the quantity the miller took his payment, which usually ranged from one-eighth to one-twelfth of the total. After grinding, sifting, and cooling the flour, the miller returned the finished product to the waiting farmer.[13]

---

11. George Rogers Taylor, *The Transportation Revolution, 1815–1860* (Armonk, NY: M. E. Sharpe, 1951), 210; Inez E. Burns, "Settlement and Early History of the Coves of Blount County, Tennessee," *East Tennessee Historical Society's Publications* 24 (1952): 53.

12. Oliver Evans, *The Young Millwright and Miller's Guide* (Philadelphia: self-published, 1795); Eric Sloane, *Our Vanishing Landscape* (New York: Ballantine Books, 1974), 40–44; Durwood Dunn, *Cades Cove: The Life and Death of a Southern Appalachian Community, 1818–1937* (Knoxville: University of Tennessee Press, 1988), 81; John Storck and Walter D. Teague, *Flour for Man's Bread* (Minneapolis: University of Minnesota Press, 1952), 107.

13. For information on the processes of flour milling in nineteenth-century America, see Charles B. Kuhlman, *The Development of the Flour-Milling Industry in the United States* (Boston: Houghton Mifflin, 1929), 94.

Figure 49. The vertical wheel (*top, left*) utilized in Cable's Mill, Cades Cove, is propelled with water over the top (overshot wheel); wheels propelled by water from the bottom are called undershot wheels. A mill race (*top, right*) directed the flow of water to the mill wheel. The Alfred Reagan "tub" or "tubbin" (from the word, turbine) mill (*bottom, right*) is a horizontal wheel propelled from water current passing its blades or compartments. The shaft from the turbine transferred motion directly to the mill's grinding stones (*bottom, left*). Photograph (*top, left*) archived at the Great Smoky Mountains National Park (GSMNP-80235-9) and photographs (*top, right, and bottom*) courtesy of Michael Angst.

Over time many local residents engaged in milling. James Gillespy, a local doctor, operated a mill near Kinzel Springs. William Myers owned a mill on the Little River, and Willie Lequire had a cotton gin attached to his flourmill. Although there is no historical record of cotton being grown in Tuckaleechee Cove in the 1800s, someone must have been producing it. Lequire undoubtedly sensed the potential for profit before building the gin, which remained in business until the early 1900s.[14]

Increased traffic to mills spurred local road development and attracted artisans and merchants. After John Walker received permission to build a mill in Tuckaleechee Cove, the county government ordered him and other local men to build a public road from Walker's mill to another mill on Pistol Creek in Maryville. Although Walker's mill was never completed, the road to Maryville was built. Other roads were built to Cades Cove and Sevierville.[15]

New roads and prosperous mills also attracted a variety of craftsmen who worked in conjunction with the miller. Coopers and blacksmiths built barrels and casks, and dry-good merchants sold finished products to local residents. Merchants took advantage of the commercial traffic created by mills in Tuckaleechee Cove. Alex M. Kennedy, a mechanic, and Jefferson Stone, a physician, lived and worked near Peter Rule's mill, and Samuel Rowan's tannery and George Snider's general store were located close to Absalom Abbott's mill.[16]

Religious Life in Tuckaleechee Cove

At the same time they were learning how to earn a living, early residents of Tuckaleechee Cove concentrated on the social and cultural growth of the community. Religion was the core of the area's culture. In 1799 Presbyterians met at Eusebia, east of the cove, to plan a church in Tuckaleechee Cove and petition for the necessary supplies to hold services. Although the church was never built, the Presbytery sent Gideon Blackburn "to supply one Sabbath at least at Tuckaleechy & as many week days as practicable & catechize one day there before our next stated Sessions." In 1803 the Tennessee Association of Baptists recommended building a church in the cove under the stewardship of William Davis and James Taylor. After a twenty-year lull, a new wave of church construction began on May 1, 1830, when the Little River Circuit of the Methodist Episcopal Church began servicing parishioners in the four nearby coves—Tuckaleechee, Cades, Millers, and Wears Coves. By 1832 the circuit's popularity led to a new church known as "the Campgrounds." Built under the direction of Frederick Emert, and on his land, neighbors helped make the Campgrounds an important part of Tuckaleechee's religious community.[17]

---

14. Burns, *History of Blount County*, 224.

15. Blount County Court Minutes, Deed Book I (1801), 153; Burns, *Blount County*, 46; *History of Tennessee* (Chicago: Goodspeed Publishing, 1887), 828–29. The road was constructed with help from John Walker Jr., John Walker Sr., Alexander Montgomery, John Bradley, Alexander Miller, William Cowan, John Craig, Samuel Thompson, Joseph Colville, George Colville, and George Snider.

16. Burns, *History of Blount County*, 46–51

17. Ibid., 49–51

In 1834 the Tuckaleechee Baptist Church opened and then reorganized in 1839 after the congregation divided over the church's mission. Also in 1839 the new Bethel Baptist Church created a covenant of fifteen foundational beliefs, nominated William Walker as its leader, and appointed William Adams pastor of the congregation. That year Baptists in Tuckaleechee sent delegates to conferences in nearby Wears Valley and Beaver Ridge and to larger ones in Knoxville and Nashville. In 1860 Tuckaleechee Baptist members resolved that they needed a larger church. George Snider, a local merchant, donated $100 and provided twelve pounds of nails for the project. John Walker and John Myers provided ceiling planks; Eli Caylor donated sealing material and weatherboarding; George Caylor, T. J. Freshour, and George Freshour gave construction material; and T. J. Wear made his sawmill available to cut lumber.[18]

The authority of churches can be seen in how members regulated the actions of individual parishioners. Foul language or lack of participation brought punishment that ranged from minor fines to full expulsion. In 1843 Ann Brickey of Bethel Baptist Church was dismissed from the parish for "not taking the gospel steps" with the Pastor Adams and for making false statements. Even the Reverend Adams was accused of "false swearing," but no witnesses came forward and the charges were dropped. In 1862 Baptists expelled five men at one time for intoxication.[19]

The Expansion of Business in Tuckaleechee Cove, 1830–1860

In the middle of the 1800s, Tuckaleechee Cove benefited from economic growth in East Tennessee and its proximity to Maryville. Blount County had rich farmland, deposits of iron and marble, and good road connections to Knoxville. By 1834 Maryville had almost six hundred residents, among them four lawyers, four clergymen, three physicians, and a wide assortment of craftsmen. The town had three churches, five stores, two taverns, three gristmills, and a printing office. It also was home to the South Western Theological Seminary, which had three professors, twenty-two students, and a library. Starting in 1832, the United States Post Office provided regular mail service between Maryville, Sevierville, and Tuckaleechee Cove. In 1836 Blount County created seventeen civil districts, and Tuckaleechee Cove composed most of the Fifteenth District. The county's taxable property was diverse and broad-based in the middle of the 1800s. See table 3 for information on property in Blount County. Note that the Fifteenth District had few slaves but more than its share of gristmills and distilleries.[20]

18. Tuckaleechee Baptist Church members in 1839 included William Walker, Nancy Caylor, Elizabeth Walker, Elizabeth Headrick, Polly Headrick, John Meyers, Elizabeth Meyers, Yancy Thurman Sr., Yancy Thurman Jr., Jane Walt, Carolyn Spence, Ann Brickey, Charley Walker, Hetty Walker, Salina Smith, George Caylor, Nancy Law, and Gary Rix. Among those who donated money in 1860 were Jacob Freshour, Joseph Walker, Levi Dunn, L. P. Dunn, George Caylor, E. Harvey, Eli Caylor, George Freshour, Daniel Dunn, Daniel Headrick, John Walker, T. J. Wear, Thomas Henry, William Walker, Tyre Walker, Daniel Caylor, A. Tipton, William Myers, John Myers, John Caylor Sr., George Fann, Henry Webb, and George Snider. This analysis is based on *Bethel Baptist Church, Townsend, Tennessee, 1840–1924*, Publication No. 2051, Historical Commission of the Southern Baptist Convention, Nashville, TN.

19. Ibid.

20. Eastin Morris, *The Tennessee Gazetteer* (Nashville: Hasell Hunt, 1834), 200; Burns, "Settlement and Early History of the Coves of Blount County," 53; Burns, *History of Blount County*, 41.

TABLE 3. PERSONAL PROPERTY SUBJECT TO TAXATION, PER CIVIL DISTRICT, BLOUNT COUNTY, 1856.

District	Slaves	Gristmills	Saw Mills	Distilleries	Households
1	47	3	2	1	83
2	31	3	2	1	100
3	24	2	2	2	87
4	15	1	2	0	105
5	37	2	2	0	71
6	22	2	1	0	87
7	13	3	3	1	76
8	6	1	4	0	103
9	101	2	3	3	153
10	103	2	3	0	132
11	60	2	2	0	106
12	56	2	2	0	78
13	31	2	2	1	110
14	20	5	2	0	85
15	3	4	1	2	98
16	1	2	3	0	30
17	4	3	3	3	37
Total	**577**	**42**	**38**	**16**	**1,529***

*Table statistics are from *The East Tennessean*, July 17, 1857 (Maryville, Tennessee).

At any one time, there were several merchants in Tuckaleechee Cove, and most were said to do "tolerably well in a small way." The cove's most prominent merchant, and perhaps its richest man, was George Snider, who according to the 1850 federal census owned a 216-acre farm, two slaves, ninety head of livestock, and three hundred bushels of corn and sixty bushels of wheat in storage. Reports collected by R. G. Dun and Company, a national credit agency, highlighted Snider's increasing wealth and influence. In 1850 Dun noted Snider's past mistakes with money but believed that "he was no longer a credit risk, and as a new shop owner had become 'prudent' and stood on safe ground." Taking note of Snider's good marriage and scrupulous personal habits, Dun's correspondent thought that he had "learned in the school of experience" and would "pay a small debt as readily as any man." From March 1850 to March 1861 Snider prospered. In 1860 the census taker reported that he owned $10,000 in real estate and $9,500 in personal property. But the Civil War disrupted business in all its forms for George Snider and his community. Snider closed his store, and by 1870 his real estate holdings were worth only $6,000, and his personal property had plummeted to $2,130. Some of the decline no doubt came from the emancipation of his slaves. By 1869, however, Snider had reopened his store and began to recoup what he had lost. His net worth eventually reached $50,000, and Dun agents deemed him a "very desirable customer."[21]

In the 1840s an iron industry emerged in Tuckaleechee Cove to take advantage of ore deposits in the mountains nearby. Robert Shield owned a bloomery forge, a small oven in which iron ore was heated with charcoal. Built in 1843 Shield's bloomery remained active until a flood washed it away. George Amerine owned a bloomery forge in nearby Millers Cove. Built in 1845 and located on Hess's Creek, Amerine's forge had two bloomery fires and a water-powered hammer. By 1856 it produced fifteen tons of iron.[22]

Residents of Tuckaleechee Cove thus pursued various nonagricultural occupations. The 1850 census listed Peter Rule and Absolom Abbott as millers, Samuel Rowan as a tanner, and Joseph Sims as a mechanic. Jefferson Stone was the only local physician. By 1860 John and Robert McCampbell and Thomas Wear had become millers, William Fann made baskets, and William Peterson toiled as a blacksmith. See table 4 for a summary of occupations taken from ten federal censuses between 1850 and 1930. Many local farmers had informal secondary occupations or skills not listed in the census. Almost all the rural inhabitants had skills or talents that contributed to their livelihoods. Together these crafts created a well-rounded community that was mostly, but not completely, self-sufficient in the 1800s.

TABLE 4. BREAKDOWN OF OCCUPATIONS PER HEAD OF HOUSEHOLD, TUCKALEECHEE COVE, 1850–1930.

Year	Agriculture	Commerce	Industry	Professional	Railroad
1850	88	3	3	1	0
1860	97	4	3	2	0
1870	158	0	0	1	0
1880	48	2	2	1	0
1890	n/a	n/a	n/a	n/a	n/a[24]
1900	156	4	0	2	0
1910	165	12	80	4	27
1920	193	14	48	2	14
1930	59	21	163	7	34
Total	**965**	**60**	**299**	**20**	**75**

Source: United States Federal Census, 1850–1930.

21. "Blount County, Tennessee," R. G. Dun and Company, 1850, Harvard University School of Business Library, Cambridge, MA.

22. J. P. Lesley, *The Iron Manufacturer's Guide to the Furnaces, Forges, and Rolling Mills of the United States* (New York: John Wiley, 1859), 202.

Census records provide good insight into the makeup of an entire community, but they do not offer as much individual detail as probated wills and estate inventories. To the 1850 census taker, for example, Samuel Walker looked like most residents of Tuckaleechee Cove. He owned one hundred acres of improved land and five hundred acres of unimproved land along the banks of the Little River, three horses, two milk cows, two head of cattle, fifteen sheep, and forty-five hogs with a sizable crop of corn in storage. In 1850 he valued his farm at $2,000 and his livestock at $450. But when he died in 1859, his will bequeathed his wife, Rebecca, $600 and the rest of his estate until her death, at which time Walker's remaining property was to be divided among family members. The will revealed that Walker owned two farms and held the titles to undeveloped land parcels totaling more than two hundred acres. He decreed in his will that his daughter, Sarah Henry, should receive a clock, $25 in cash, some cattle, a horse, six hogs, and a cook stove. One grandson received 150 acres of farmland and cash, while another grandson got a smaller parcel of land, blacksmith tools, and part of the proceeds from a livestock auction. One of Walker's granddaughters received a substantial piece of land, a wagon, and farm tools, and another a one-sixth share of his estate and some furniture. Walker concluded his will by giving his brother, Vance Walker, his joiner tools, anvil and bellows, crosscut saw, and some money. The will gave a brief description and estimated value for every item in Walker's estate. Although these records do not provide a description of his home, the inventory provides a general sense of his modest wealth. Walker and his wife slept in a bed with a headboard, cooked in a big kettle over a manufactured cook stove, kept time with a clock worth $9.50, and owned a small collection of books. No decorations, paintings, or furniture other than those for the bedroom and kitchen were listed. For a man of Walker's wealth and proximity to merchants in Maryville and Knoxville, he seemed to lack a materialist bent.[23]

Other Tuckaleechee Cove residents apparently enjoyed a more refined lifestyle. Peter Brickey's estate inventory reflected a man of greater social standing and economic diversity. Aside from common household items and dishware, Brickey owned thirty-five pewter plates, cups, and saucers and a pewter teapot; a sugar bowl; decorative dishes; a sundial; and candlesticks. He also owned a looking glass, clock, wood chest, three beds with furniture, five chairs, and three tables. Perhaps the differences between the two estates can be explained by what was outside their homes. Both Walker and Brickey owned relatively large, well-equipped farms in the cove. Walker's farm contained three wagons, an abundance of livestock, and large reserves of wheat and corn. Brickey's farm also had a full complement of wagons, plows, livestock, and farm implements, and he owned tools for barrel making, metal forging, milling, timbering, and general carpentry. He had the necessary equipment to harvest timber for his own use and the commercial market, including log chains, iron

23. The information on Samuel Walker and Peter Brickey is based on Blount County Inventories and Estates, vol. D (Maryville, TN), 22–23, 114–17, 274–80.

forks, a crosscut saw, axes, a hand saw, and iron wedges. With these tools he could cut and drag timber from his farm and either use it for his own work or ship it to local mills.

His will suggests that Brickey engaged in one lucrative economic activity besides farming. It listed "one still & some tubs singling and doubling kegs, all old, some good tubs." Brickey produced whiskey from corn that he or his neighbors grew, distilled the alcohol in his own still fired by wood he cut from his property, and stored the finished product in wooden kegs and barrels he shaped and assembled with his cooper's tools. These casks were probably then loaded onto wagons and driven to Maryville, Knoxville, or Sevierville.

Peter Brickey's manufacture of whiskey was an entirely legal practice at that time. Distilleries became commonplace on American farms in the 1700s. They created a political crisis for President George Washington when Pennsylvania farmers rebelled against the federal government's attempt to tax whiskey in the early 1790s. In Tuckaleechee Cove making whiskey was an accepted practice, although it later became controversial. There were strong economic motives for distilling corn into whiskey. It represented a finished product that was relatively easy to ship, as opposed to large amounts of corn that were difficult to transport. Much of East Tennessee was engaged in this commerce; newspapers carried numerous advertisements for large distilleries and often touted local varieties, such as Roane County whiskey.[24]

Estate inventories also listed debtors and creditors of the deceased. At a time when few financial institutions existed in the immediate region, neighbors created complex webs of exchanges. Samuel Walker's inventory reflects how important personal credit was. Walker held notes on many of his neighbors for various amounts. Among those who owed money to Walker were seven men, three of whom lived in Maryville and two near Tuckaleechee Cove at Gamble's Store. Walker in turn owed money to fourteen persons who lived in or near the cove. This geographic array of debtors and creditors indicates the growing interaction between residents of the cove and the rest of Blount County. Samuel Walker lived and worked in the cove but did not limit his personal or business interactions to those living in the immediate vicinity.[25]

The economic growth of Tuckaleechee Cove coincided with the overall development in Tennessee. Just as farmers, millers, craftsmen, and merchants established a vibrant economy in Tuckaleechee Cove, larger economic forces began transforming East Tennessee. Knoxville became a regional manufacturing center, commercial marketplace, and transportation hub. Railroads enabled a wider marketplace. Before the arrival of railroads in East Tennessee, farmers, industrialists, and merchants had to ship their goods on rough wagon roads or by boat on the Tennessee River. By 1858 the completion of the East Tennessee and Georgia Railroad and the East Tennessee and Virginia Railroad allowed producers and merchants to expand their geographic scope. Now a farmer in Tuckaleechee Cove could sell his produce

24. *Maryville Republican*, December 6, 1873.

25. Manuscript Census for Blount County, Tennessee, Population Schedule, Eighth Census, 1860.

or livestock to a merchant in Knoxville and have it shipped to larger markets in New York City or Baltimore or Charleston. Tuckaleechee residents now bought new things because they had better access to merchants who carried a variety of agricultural tools, household necessities, and luxury items.[26]

If the economic potential of the region seemed limitless in the late 1850s, local residents had to worry about the growing conflict between southerners and northerners over slavery. Although slavery never gained much presence in the valleys and mountains of East Tennessee, Blount County was home to 241 slaveholders and 1,363 slaves by 1860. In Tuckaleechee Cove slavery had dwindled from 13 slave owners and 58 slaves in 1850 to just 5 masters and 20 slaves in 1860. As slavery ripped the nation apart along sectional lines in the 1850s, Tuckaleechee Cove remained relatively peaceful. But soon large political and military conflicts would threaten even the peaceful and prosperous cove. The roads that had enabled that prosperity soon brought news of war, disunion, and danger.

Suggested Readings

Brown, Margaret L. *The Wild East: A Biography of the Great Smoky Mountains*. Gainesville: University Press of Florida, 2000. A recent overview of the history of the region.

Burns, Inez E. *History of Blount County, Tennessee: From War Trail to Landing Strip, 1795–1955*. Nashville: Tennessee Historical Commission, 1957. An old but authoritative account of the history of the county in which Tuckaleechee is located.

De Vorsey, Louis, Jr. *The Indian Boundary in the Southern Colonies, 1763–1775*. Chapel Hill: University of North Carolina Press, 1961. A thorough account of the crucial period of Euro- and Native American contact.

Dunn, Durwood. *Cades Cove: The Life and Death of a Southern Appalachian Community, 1818–1937*. Knoxville: University of Tennessee Press, 1988. An excellent study of a nearby community on a mountain plateau.

Rothrock, Mary U. *The French Broad–Holston Country: A History of Knox County, Tennessee*. Knoxville: East Tennessee Historical Society, 1946. The history of a neighboring, and sometimes dominant, county.

26. On outside awareness of East Tennessee's economic promise, see, for example, *De Bow's Review* (1853): 318–310. Lewis Gray, an agricultural historian, later claimed that "railway building was an important element in the economic revival [of East Tennessee], opening up sections remote from market, increasing the farm price of their products, and enabling them to achieve a great degree of commercialism." See Gray, *History of Agriculture in the Southern United States to 1860* (Washington, DC: Carnegie Institution of Washington, 1933), 882–85.

Chapter 5

THE CIVIL WAR AND ITS AFTERMATH

Many familiar faces in Tuckaleechee Cove in the 1850s had in fact migrated there from afar. Frederick Emert, for example, had been born in Pennsylvania and had made a series of moves down the Great Valley of Virginia before settling in the cove. Some who came to the cove made it only a short stop on their way to another place. The most interesting of these sojourners must have been John Mitchel, whose life was an exciting adventure with many unpredictable twists.

Born to a well-educated Protestant family in Northern Ireland, Mitchel in the 1840s adopted the Irish nationalism popular among Catholics and converted to Catholicism himself. He became a leading agitator against British rule, writing articles for a revolutionary newspaper that marked him as a traitor to British authorities. In 1848 the British in Ireland tried and convicted Mitchel of treason and sentenced him to fourteen years in an Australian prison. In 1853 he escaped, made his way to New York City, and resumed his attacks on the British government. He also took up American issues from the Irish-immigrant position. He attacked the growing anti-immigrant movement in the United States. But paradoxically for someone who fought furiously against the mistreatment of the Irish by the English, Mitchel supported slavery and opposed abolitionism. Like most of the Irish in the United States, he held strong anti-black views. Poor health eventually forced Mitchel to leave New York, and he traveled to East Tennessee.

His arrival and political views were noted in Knoxville, and soon William Brownlow, the Unionist editor of the *Knoxville Whig*, denounced him. Mitchel became editor of Knoxville's pro-secessionist newspaper, the *Southern Citizen*. A war of words about slavery, secession, states' rights, and religion then filled the pages of their competing newspapers. Brownlow, a Methodist preacher known as "Parson," held fierce anti-Catholic views and warned his readers that Mitchel's Catholic connection came "oozing out of the *Citizen's* contempt for Protestant meetings." Mitchel returned the angry rhetoric in kind. He condemned Brownlow for being "frantic in his personal abuse of all and sundry, and is generally understood to be perfectly ready to gouge any fellow-creature at a moment's notice."

Hoping to escape the hostility of Knoxville, Mitchel visited Tuckaleechee Cove and became enchanted with the idea of living a solitary, rural lifestyle. In 1855 he bought a farm in the cove. He had escaped the modern world and settled amid "immense forests and mountains, with innumerable rivers; deer, turkey, to say nothing of bears, wolves, and 'painters' [cougars]. In short I desired to fly from the turmoil of New York, and to try to see whether life might be possible for us among the woods. Other folks had found it so; why not we?"[1]

Mitchel appreciated the beauty of Tuckaleechee Cove. With characteristic Irish literary flourish, he described it to a friend: "a most lovely valley, five miles long, varying in breadth from a quarter of a mile to a mile and a half, and lying among parallel folds of the Alleghenies. Through it gushes and flashes one of the brightest and most crystalline of rivers . . . whose banks are sometimes corn-fields fringed with trees, sometimes shelves of sand, sometimes, precipices twice the height of St. George's steeple" (a Dublin church known for its tall spire). The banks of the Little River were "crowned and plumed with oaks and pines," and its water "here and there dash and rave over broken rocks, there ripple gently over a pebbly bed, arching boughs of great trees." Mitchel's farm lay "up in the nook where the river first bursts from its mountain solitudes, and its pine-shaded ravine expands into the vale of Tuckaleechee—up so high that my only neighbors are the bears and deer, I have pitched my tent." He resided higher than any other man in the valley on 132 acres, of which about 50 were cleared for cultivation. He built a log house and a large barn "just now full of the fruits of the earth, two horses, three cows, and that indispensable part of a Tennessean's stock—a multitude of pigs."

Mitchel's idyllic existence soon ended. His reputation for political radicalism and prosecessionism followed him all the way to the cove. He received word that an attorney in Blount County had alleged that the Irishman planned "to take away from the free and enlightened Americans the liberty they had acquired by their revolution." In 1856 he returned to Knoxville and resumed the debate with Brownlow. The controversy over slavery and secession escalated. Mitchel never returned to Tuckaleechee, but he eventually did go back to Ireland and won a seat in the British parliament, only to have it denied because he was a convicted felon.[2]

Tensions increased throughout East Tennessee as the political rhetoric of secession soared. By 1860 rumors of secession and war swirled in East Tennessee. In December 1860 secessionists held a rally in Maryville to oppose Abraham Lincoln and the Republican Party. Most residents of Tuckaleechee Cove remained loyal Unionists. In February 1861 East Tennessean Unionists led the defeat of secession in a statewide referendum, but secessionist forces from Middle and West Tennessee called for another referendum. In June better-organized secessionists won another vote, and Tennessee left the Union. Although far removed from state

1. Samuel C. Williams, "John Mitchel, the Irish Patriot, Resident of Tennessee," *East Tennessee Historical Society's Publications* 10 (1938): 44–56; William Dillon, *Life of John Mitchel*, 2 vols. (London: Trench, 1888), 71, 64; Blount County Deeds, book Y, 220, 223, 625.

2. Dillon, *Life of John Mitchel*, 74–76 , 85.

politics, one Tuckaleechee Cove resident, Alexander Kennedy, showed his disapproval of the second referendum by attending a Unionist convention in Knoxville to discuss recent political events. A fifty-eight-year-old mechanic and ex-slaveholder with seven children, Kennedy risked his reputation and personal wellbeing by attending the convention in secessionist Knoxville. Kennedy listened to Unionist speeches and voted on motions decrying the "ruinous and heretical doctrine of secession."[3]

Isolated deep within the boundaries of the newly formed Confederate States of America, loyal East Tennessean Union sympathizers became outcasts in their own state and country. Rumors of violence and bloodshed swirled around Blount County, and both sides braced for attacks by the other. Reports of well-armed Blount County Unionists prompted a Confederate cavalry regiment led by Colonel John H. Morgan to leave Knoxville and patrol Unionist activity. Oliver P. Temple, a Knoxville Unionist, later insisted that the presence of Confederate troops in East Tennessee encouraged "extreme arrogance" toward Union men, which increased after the South's first victory at Bull Run. In rural districts like Tuckaleechee Cove, Temple said, Confederates became especially insulting to Unionists: "Sometimes the most sacred ties of friendship and even of kinship were disregarded," and even formerly mild-mannered men seemed to become "anxious for blood."[4]

Passing Armies

If the war seemed distant to those living in the relative peace of Tuckaleechee Cove, the events of June 1861 brought the potential for violence and disruption much closer to home. Unionist residents of Tuckaleechee Cove and nearby communities held a mass rally on the muster grounds near the Little River at Walland Gap, at the west end of Tuckaleechee Cove. More than 1,500 attended the rally and hoisted an American flag. A Confederate cavalry unit, on its way to the cove to collect firearms from potential union partisans, stopped at the muster ground to remove the American flag, but the Confederates let it fly, and moved on. News of the flag episode spread quickly, and the cavalry's act may have averted an ambush. Instead of attacking, local Union partisans hid their weapons and waited for the Confederates to leave the area.

William Brownlow's belligerent nature and inflammatory articles made Knoxville unsafe for him in 1861. He first moved to Maryville but was soon on the run again after being accused of arson. The reputation of Tuckaleechee Cove as a Unionist sanctuary enticed Parson Brownlow and other Unionists from East Tennessee to hide in relative safety in the ridges above the cove.[5]

3. W. Todd Groce, *Mountain Rebels: East Tennessee Confederates and the Civil War, 1860–1870* (Knoxville: University of Tennessee Press, 1999), 25, 39; Robert T. McKenzie, *Lincolnites and Rebels: A Divided Town in the American Civil War* (New York: Oxford University Press, 2006), 58–60, 79–81; Burns, *Blount County*, 316.

4. Oliver P. Temple, *East Tennessee and the Civil War* (Cincinnati, OH: Robert Clarke, 1899), 367.

5. Burns, "Settlement and Early History of the Coves of Blount County," 59–60; E. Merton Coulter, *William G. Brownlow: Fighting Parson of the Southern Highlands* (1937; repr., Knoxville: University of Tennessee Press, 1999), 182.

Confederate leaders sent thousands of troops to East Tennessee to try to quash Unionism. In addition to regular troops, wandering groups of Confederate vigilantes made the situation tense for those who had previously proclaimed their loyalty to the Union. The young men of Tuckaleechee Cove, undoubtedly excited and nervous about the war, had to find alternative ways to join the Union army early in the war. In 1862 Daniel and John Caylor, sons of a prominent Tuckaleechee farmer, were fearful of Confederate vigilantes but eager to fight for their cause. The Caylors left under the cover of darkness and, helped by other Unionists, joined up with a unit at the Cumberland Gap in Kentucky. There the Caylors mustered into the Sixth Tennessee Volunteer Infantry, which contained many men who had escaped the East Tennessee Confederates. Over the course of the war, the unit participated in battles at Nashville, Chickamauga, and Knoxville and took part in Sherman's campaign in Atlanta. John Caylor fought until he was wounded at the Battle of Marietta in July 1864. He rejoined his company the following December, and he and Daniel served until the end of the war.[6]

By late 1862 the threat of Confederate retribution had declined to the point that Union Colonel D. M. Ray traveled to Maryville and openly called for men to join his troop. Nine men from Tuckaleechee Cove answered this call and enlisted in Company D of the Second Tennessee Volunteers. They included four from the Brewer family, two each from the Walkers and Brickeys, and Levi Dunn. For the next two and a half years, they experienced the tedium of camp life, the excitement of battle, and fear of injury, sickness, and death. Company D spent much of its first year in and around Nashville, but by May 1864 the unit had moved to Woodville and then Decatur, Alabama, to chase Confederate forces led by cavalry generals Joseph Wheeler and Nathan Bedford Forrest. After months in the field, the unit was transferred to the relative safety of Vicksburg, Mississippi, and from January to April 1865, Company D remained bivouacked seven miles outside the port city before making its way back to Tennessee.[7]

Company D escaped the tragedies that marked the war experience, with one exception. A month before the end of the war, Joseph Walker, an illiterate tenant farmer in his mid-twenties, received a fatal gunshot wound at Paducah, Kentucky. He left his wife a small plot of land and seventy-five dollars' worth of personal possessions. In July 1865 the eight surviving men from Tuckaleechee Cove mustered out of the Union army in Nashville and made their way home. William Brewer had emerged as a dependable soldier and received a promotion to sergeant in 1863, but for reasons unknown, William Brickey was demoted from corporal to private, while James C. Brewer was branded a deserter after leaving his unit

---

6. Will A. McTeer, John Andes, and Charles S. McCammon, *Loyal Mountain Troopers: the Second and Third Tennessee Volunteer Cavalry in the Civil War; Reminiscences of Lieutenant John W. Andes and Major Will A.* McTeer (Maryville, TN : Blount County Genealogical and Historical Society, 1992), 49–53; Janet B. Hewett, ed., *Supplement to the Official Records of the Union and Confederate Armies, Part II—Records of Events*, vol. 65, serial no. 77 (Wilmington, NC: Broadfoot, 1998), 758–59; National Archives and Records Service, *Compiled Service Records of Volunteer Union Soldiers Who Served in Organizations From the State of Tennessee*, Sixth Infantry, C–E (Washington, D.C.: National Archives and Records Service, 1962), Roll 167, microfilm.

7. Hewitt, *Supplement to the Official Records*, vol. 65: 758–59.

in October 1863. Although he eventually returned to his unit, Brewer lost back pay and had the incident placed on his permanent service record. Perhaps aware of the partisan violence that continued to grip East Tennessee after the Confederate surrender, Levi Dunn asked to retain his service revolver.[8]

For those residents who did not join the military, the war became a pressing reality when forces from both sides entered Tuckaleechee Cove in 1863 and 1864. In December 1863 General William Tecumseh Sherman moved through the area and camped in Maryville on his way to relieve General Ambrose Burnside's troops in Knoxville. His troops spread across the county. During the last years of the war, Confederate partisans scattered and harassed residents of Tuckaleechee Cove.

In response to Confederate vigilantes, the communities in the cove organized a Home Guard to protect against raids and attacks. The Home Guard maintained peace in the cove for much of the war. But when regular army troops were in the area, the Home Guard stayed clear. In early 1864 the First Kentucky Cavalry, under the command of Colonel Frank Wolford, attacked a local Confederate unit at nearby Kelley's Ford. After nearly two hours of fighting, Wolford ordered his troops to withdraw through Tuckaleechee Cove. Confederate troops did not pursue, and the First Kentucky made it safely back to Maryville. The next day Brigadier General S. D. Sturgis reported another day of heavy cavalry fighting in the area, and like Wolford, he was forced to retreat to Tuckaleechee Cove. While Sturgis's men set up camp, he received news that a "force of Indians and whites commanded by the rebel Thomas was near the forks of Little Tennessee and Tuckaseegee Rivers in North Carolina, [and] had become a terror to the Union people of East Tennessee." Sturgis ordered a detachment of his troops to scout the area and engage the enemy if necessary, and they soon drove the Confederates from Tuckaleechee Cove.[9]

Reconstructing Peace

After four years of war, much of the South lay in ruin. Campaigning armies had burned homes and barns, killed livestock, destroyed fences, twisted railroad tracks, and rutted roads

8. National Archives, *Compiled Service Records of Volunteer Union Soldiers;* Manuscript Census, 1860, Blount County Eighth Census.

9. Orlando M. Poe, *Occupation of East Tennessee and the Defense of Knoxville* (Detroit, MI: Ostler Printing, 1889), 44); Burns, *Blount County*, 318–19; United States War Department, *The War of the Rebellion: A Compilation of the Official Records of the Union and Confederate Armies* (1891; repr., Gettysburg, PA: National Historical Society, 1972), ser. 1, vol. 32, pt. 1: 55; Hewett, *Supplement to the Official Records*, vol. 30: 139, 176, 190. A muster Roll of the Home Guard, Fifteenth Civil District, February 18, 1865, included these men: Jacob Bird, E. A. Gregory, Daniel Headrick, L. P. Dunn, J. P. Dunn, William Walker, Nathan Sparks, Jonas Jenkins, John Meyers Sr., William Oliver, Joseph Lukewire, D. H. Meyers, H. N. Tipton, J. W. R. Harrison, M. Cameron, Nathaniel Burchfield, David Wadkins, David Webb, W. P. Dunn, A. G. Dunn, D. L. Bird, Philip David, Henry Web, J. A. Bowers, E. M. McCampbell, C. S. Fancher, I. W. Lukewire, J. H. Gregory, W. L. Welch, Peter Burchfield, J. A. Shields, Thomas B. Chambers, James Shields, N. A. Miller, W. M. Dunn, J. E. Chambers, J. W. Lane, Thomas Henry, Joel Johnston, and E. R. W. Bird.

throughout the South. In the postwar years, violence still plagued much of East Tennessee. If war had settled the question of slavery, it had not soothed sectional disagreements, and many northerners wanted to punish the South for causing the war. In much of Tennessee, the end of formal military operations brought little relief for residents. Homes, churches, schools, businesses, and governmental offices that had been closed or destroyed during the war now struggled to begin operating. Murder, rape, and robbery became common as bands of criminals and vigilantes roamed the area. To resume the upward economic trends of the 1850s, East Tennesseans first had to restore law and order and then repair the physical damage done by war and initiate better relationships with northerners. Sustained economic growth required the intersectional cooperation that had been destroyed in 1861. For East Tennessee, this meant reestablishing railroad connections and investing in infrastructure. Despite a common desire for peace and economic prosperity, it would take years to overcome personal grudges and sectional loyalties.[10]

In Tuckaleechee Cove war damage had been minimal. In comparison to other areas in East Tennessee and the South, the cove saw little military action. Despite ominous threats, farmers had continued to plant and harvest their fields, church doors remained open, and stores stayed in business. Soldiers had left home to fight for their cause, and one had died for his beliefs; but as the survivors returned, they found a community touched by war but easily recognizable to their weary eyes. Passing armies had trampled the land and foraged in the fields and forests of Tuckaleechee Cove, but its strong natural defenses had protected it from worse damage. The incidents of bushwhacking and attacks motivated by personal vendettas that plagued many East Tennessee communities for years after the war apparently did not occur in Tuckaleechee Cove. Families wanted to put the hardships of the war behind them. Farmers began planting crops and mending neglected fences and barns. Their sense of community was the foundation for recovery and renewed growth. By 1869 one observer reported that "all is quiet in the coves."[11]

The people of Tuckaleechee Cove had much to do. Neglected roads were repaired in July 1865 when the county government appointed Marion Cameron to rehabilitate the road from Tuckaleechee Cove to Maryville in the west. Cameron and the county government expected local farmers to help with the work and specifically named each man or family along the route. The list included thirteen men and five women, two of them widows. County officials also instructed Jacob Freshour to oversee improvements to the road to Sevierville to the east, with help from sixteen men, including most of the veterans of Company D, and two widows. These roads, as much as any crop or business, were instrumental in reestablishing trade between Tuckaleechee Cove and Maryville and Sevierville. Without good roads, farmers would be unable to sell their produce or buy goods from merchants in the larger commercial centers.[12]

10. Stephen Ash, *Middle Tennessee, Society Transformed, 1860–1870* (Baton Rogue: Louisiana State University Press,1988), 175–81.

11. *Maryville Record*, November 23, 1869.

12. Blount County Court Minutes, July 1865, 50–51, McClung Collection, Knox County Public Library, Knoxville, TN.

The war had little influence on the agricultural habits of Tuckaleechee Cove farmers. Farmers continued to grow wheat, rye, and corn and to raise hogs and cattle. But there was a significant shift in the patterns of land tenure: more farmers rented their land than had done so prior to the war. The 1860 census records indicate that forty-six men owned their farms and fifty men rented land. By 1870 tenancy numbers had almost doubled to ninety-nine renters and fifty-nine farm owners. Unlike many other areas in the South, however, higher tenancy rates indicated an expanding population, not economic decline. Between 1860 and 1870, only seven men went from being landowners to renters. The increase in tenancy came mostly among families who moved to the area after the war, or from sons who rented land from their fathers.

The Sounds of Progress

In postwar Tuckaleechee Cove, many farmers looked for new sources of income. The older crafts of flour and corn milling, beekeeping, and whiskey distilling continued. Others began to cut timber on their property and to sell the lumber to neighbors and merchants. Cutting timber had always been a part of rural culture, but postwar entrepreneurs expanded logging activity in Tuckaleechee Cove to new levels (figure 50). The postwar demand for lumber soared, stimulating local production. Early evidence of this commercial growth emerged in the 1870s. Loggers Duncan and Harry McDonald cut large amounts of poplar and oak at John Myers's farm and other nearby areas and then shipped the wood to large commercial mills located outside the cove. A decade later, the Tuckaleechee Timber and Boom Company also began to harvest large stands of trees in the area. This new growth spurred new calls for more road improvements. In 1886 a writer for the *Maryville Times* suggested that a modern stone road between Maryville and Tuckaleechee and adjacent coves would attract railroad development. A railroad would in turn "double the trade of both and add thousands of dollars every year to the people who live on the line of road or near it, as they could bring in their grain, vegetables, fruit, lumber, &c., in double or triple the quantities they do now." At this point, a railroad was a hope, not a reality.[13]

As the timber industry grew in the late 1800s, the Little River provided loggers with the most efficient means for getting timber to sawmills (figure 51). As a boy in the late 1800s, Roy M. Myers of Tuckaleechee Cove watched as logs floated past his home after a nearby dam had been opened to create a deeper flow of water. Early commercial loggers used axes and saws to cut hardwoods and draft animals to drag the fallen timber down to the river. Winding its way through the cove in a northwesterly direction before emptying into the Tennessee River south of Knoxville, the river floated timber to sawmills in Rockford, Tennessee. Aided by dams they made and by spring freshets, loggers flooded the waterway.

13. Burns, "Settlement and Early History of the Coves of Blount County," 56; Burns, *Blount County*, 272, 230; Robert S. Lambert, "Logging on Little River, 1890–1940," *East Tennessee Historical Society's Publications* 33 (1961): 33; *Maryville Times*, February 10, 1886; Carroll Van West, ed., *The Tennessee Encyclopedia of History and Culture* (Nashville: Rutledge Hill Press, 1998), 367–68.

When low water made it impossible to float logs on the Little River, loggers brought small portable sawmills to the fallen timber and trimmed it before loading it onto waiting wagons. Seasonal log drives continued until the arrival of a railroad.[14]

The availability of milled lumber—that is, logs trimmed and cut into standard lengths and widths—altered building styles in Tuckaleechee Cove. In the 1880s the traditional log home gave way to framed constructions. At that time, mass-produced nails, new building techniques, and knowledgeable carpenters made constructing a framed home more economical and efficient. Log homes were not immediately abandoned, but new houses were typically built in the new style. The archaeological excavations in Tuckaleechee uncovered many more mass-produced, or "cut" nails, from the late 1800s than they did the older forged iron nails.

Outsiders began to take notice of Tuckaleechee Cove's growth. After the Civil War, many villages and towns published historical and biographical compilations as a way of increasing commercial visibility. General descriptions typically emphasized a place's economic features

Figure 50. Workers sitting on lumber milled at Townsend, 1910–20. (Hooks Collection, Great Smoky Mountains National Park, III-L-17032, GRSM-32771.)

14. Lambert, "Logging on Little River, 1890–1940," 32–35; Vic Weals, *Last Train to Elkmont: A Look Back at Life on Little River in the Great Smoky Mountains* (Knoxville, TN: Olden Press, 1993), 1–2.

Figure 51. Up Little River from below Tuckaleechee Cove, August 16, 1886. (Copyright © 2006. The University of Tennessee Libraries. All Rights Reserved.)

and the efforts of prominent men. For Tennessee *Goodspeed's History of Tennessee* was the standard for this genre of literature. In 1887 *Goodspeed's* noted the importance of the Little River and the businesses it supported, specifically mentioning John Walker's mill and George Snider's general store.[15]

Newspapers also made it their business to promote the economy of the regions where they were published. In 1878 S. Z. Sharp of the *Maryville Index* traveled to Tuckaleechee Cove and then along the Little River into the "rugged and romantic" landscape of the area.

15. *Goodspeed's History of Tennessee,* 1887.

With the nearby Smoky Mountains standing like a "giant guardian," Sharp noted "beautiful bottoms of the richest soil . . . along the banks of the river, while the upland is naturally good, being improved by a very pure kind of limestone." After a full day of traveling, he accepted the "generous hospitality of Col. Tipton, and enjoyed the kindness of his estimable wife and the society of his two talented daughters." Tipton and Sharp spent the next day touring the area, including two local schools where Sharp was "delighted with the intelligent faces of the pupils and the interest manifested by the people in building good school houses and keeping good schools."[16]

That night Tipton went to church with the Sharp family and other local residents. Church membership in Tuckaleechee Cove grew as new people moved into the area after the Civil War. The number of members reached 164 in 1880, and it would grow to 347 in 1902 after the influx of new workers at the Little River Lumber Company. Church members devoted much time to the physical upkeep of their church buildings, which served many purposes beyond worship services. Parishioners took particular pride in the outward appearance of their sanctuary.

Tuckaleechee churches continued to monitor closely the behavior of their members. Members of the Primitive Baptist Church of Christ sometimes faced sanctions from elders for violating community standards. For example, in 1873 Powell Fry lost his membership in the church after being accused of disorderly conduct, lying, cursing, using the Lord's name in vain, and being drunk. Also "turned out" out of the church were Levi Henry, J. W. D. Brickey, and George Rice for being drunk in public. But elders also rendered mercy. When Mary Abbott confessed her faults and asked for forgiveness for her "imprudent conduct" in 1875, she received forgiveness from the congregation and was allowed to continue attending services. Some breaches of morality were unforgivable, however, and in separate incidents in 1878 and 1887, two women lost their church membership after living simultaneously with more than one man.[17]

Occasional natural disasters marked the history of Tuckaleechee Cove in the late 1800s. In 1875 a flood washed away Henry Webb's home, destroyed a number of smaller homes and buildings, and carried away large amounts of fencing. Local farmers estimated that enough fencing had been deposited on John Rorax's farm to enclose all of Blount County. The flood disrupted business in the cove and nearby communities, causing an estimated $150,000 in damage. Almost as disruptive were personal feuds that resulted in violence. In 1883 at Daniel Emmett's general store, an argument between Levi W. Dunn, veteran of Company D and now a prominent farmer and father of five, and Joseph E. Scott, a tenant farmer, escalated to the point that Dunn stabbed Scott. Although the wounds were not fatal, the incident shocked local residents.[18]

---

16. *Maryville Index*, December 4, 1878.

17. Betty R. Davis, "Records of the Primitive Baptist Church of Christ in Tuckaleechee Cove, Tennessee, April 1870–August 1912" (manuscript, 1988), 15, 21, 25, 27, 40, 67, in McClung Collection, Knox County Public Library, Knoxville, TN.

18. *Maryville Record*, March 6, 1875; *East Tennessee News*, September 17, 1883.

By the late 1800s, the first-generation settlers who had cleared the land and created a sense of community had died. Second- and third-generation residents, the children and grandchildren of those original settlers, often continued their families' presence and influence in the cove. They also welcomed many newcomers to the area. The experiences of the first settlers became folklore for the later residents. One example was William B. Bird, who came to the cove from Greene County, North Carolina, not long after he was born in 1811. Bird married Susan Campbell in 1833. Although Bird was never more than a modest farmer on a 160-acre place, his relative success allowed him to spend his life in Tuckaleechee Cove without major incident or setback. He and his wife grew enough wheat and corn and raised enough livestock to meet the needs of their family. They raised ten children. They watched over their neighbors, according to the scriptural command, and continued to live on their farm until their deaths in the late 1800s. Proud that each child received a good education, William Bird watched as his descendants settled in the cove and produced fifty-three grandchildren and eighteen great-grandchildren before he died.

"Tang"

In the 1800s, residents of the cove thought of their community not as a name on a map but as their personal and collective point of reference. An outsider might have seen little to distinguish the people of the cove from those in Maryville or Wears Valley or Cades Cove, but they saw themselves as different and unique. This pride and sense of uniqueness was captured in a poem entitled "Tang," which was their slang name for Tuckaleechee Cove. Written in 1893 by a local poet called "J-N-O"—but whose actual identity is lost to the historical record—and published in the *Maryville Times,* the poem begins by taking a good-natured jab at the lack of local coverage by the newspaper and offers a number of reasons why it deserves more:

'Tis seldom a letter
    From this place you see
The cause of this
    Is a wonder to me.

Among so many men
    Great, honest and true
And college boys plentiful
    With little to do.

It seems that a letter,
    Each week should appear
Full of items of interest,
    From both, far and near.

There are incidents numerous
    From mountain to station,
And someone to work
    At every occupation.

The poet then describes many of the prominent social and cultural institutions in Tuckaleechee Cove. The role of church is in the forefront as the poem continues:

Of churches there are four,
All prosperous and strong.
In harmony and love,
They are moving along.

And with preachers we are blest,
They are as numerous as the rabbit.
There are Adams, Hamilton, Brickey
Henry, Tittsworth and Abbott.

There are two Sunday Schools,
Which success fully stand.
I love to see them prosper,
"God Bless the little band."

Any singing-masters? Yes.
I'll name them to a man,
There are Adams, Uncle Headrick,
Thomas Lawson and Dan.

The growing importance of education and medicine is highlighted as well:

And our school teachers for '93
I'll just mention for fun,
Rambo and Adams,
Josie Tipton and Ella Dunn.

Our penmen are gone,
At least it has been said,
The officers took one,
And the other is dead.

Any doctors? There are two,
They move with a hustle,
Their names are familiar,
Joe Jenkins and Russell

The writer takes a more wistful look at the commercial and governmental development in Tuckaleechee Cove:

Of merchants there are four.
All keep a good stock,
They are: Hunter, Emert,
Bill Bird and Doc.

We have two squires,
Who work for the "mon"

I am sure you know them,
They are: Jenkins and Dunn.

The sheriffs are two,
The deputy and short
A man can get to Carolina,
Before they will start.

The farmers are numerous,
But generous in deeds,
They go off a hunting,
And leave their corn in the weeds.

The Postmasters? Two.
But they are generally out,
You can get your mail,
Where there's any children about.

Any school-directors? Three.
A straight Democratic board,
They'll employ their hobbies,
And you need not say a word.

And the millers are so numerous,
You can scarcely get about.
They are: Abbott, Sam Compton
And Cool Yearout.

And of hunters there is one
Who always leads the gang.
His right name is Myres,
But we all call him "Shang."

And traders? So many
'Tis us almost absurd.
The most notable of which
Is Mr. Warren Bird.

Although written in jest, the poem captures the closeness and growth of the community, and in perhaps an attempt to pacify those left out, the writer closes:

If any one reads this,
And then wants to pout,
First understand this,
'Tis not for a flout.

But only to suit
The place and the time,
And with preceding words,
To finish a rhyme.

And now if the writer,
        You think you must know,
Do not be mistaken,
        My name is—J-N-O.

Aside from the levity and creativity of "Tang," the poem provides insight into the community. The institutions of religion, education, and business held the Tuckaleechee Cove community together. Many of the names mentioned in the poem had been a part of Tuckaleechee Cove since the early 1800s. The lyric reflected the moment in which it was written: 1893. If this poem had been written ten years later, many of the verses would have included stanzas about a new town, an outside corporation, and a railroad.

Suggested Readings

Andes, John W. *Loyal Mountain Troopers: The Second and Third Tennessee Volunteer Cavalry in the Civil War; Reminiscences of Lieutenant John W. Andes and Major Will A. McTeer*. Maryville, TN: Blount County Genealogical and Historical Society, 1992. The best primary source on the military history of the Civil War in East Tennessee.

Ash, Stephen. *Middle Tennessee, Society Transformed, 1860–1870*. Baton Rouge: Louisiana State University Press, 1988. Excellent context on the impact of the Civil War in Tennessee.

Coulter, E. Merton. *William G. Brownlow: Fighting Parson of the Southern Highlands*. Knoxville: University of Tennessee Press, 1937. An old standard on East Tennessee's most colorful and controversial Civil War political figure.

Groce, W. Todd. *Mountain Rebels: East Tennessee Confederates and the Civil War, 1860–1870*. Knoxville: University of Tennessee Press, 1999. Another good secondary source on the Civil War's impact on East Tennessee.

McKenzie, Robert T. *Lincolnites and Rebels: A Divided Town in the American Civil War*. New York: Oxford University Press, 2006. A good account of internal conflict among Tennesseans in the Civil War.

West, Carroll Van, ed. *The Tennessee Encyclopedia of History and Culture*. Nashville: Rutledge Hill Press, 1998. A wealth of information on all things Tennessean. It is now available online at http://tennesseeencyclopedia.net/.

Chapter 6

BIG INDUSTRY ON THE LITTLE RIVER

The Little River Lumber Company

The 1900s brought changes to Tuckaleechee Cove that both strengthened and loosened communal bonds. In 1906 a witness noted that "this quiet valley, so long unmolested, has yielded to the intrusion of commerce and now is heard the screech of the locomotive's warning whistle and the buzz of the rip saw, cutting the material for building the homes and palaces of the city." The witness was referring to the arrival of the Little River Lumber Company and the Little River Railroad Company and the creation of Townsend, a mill town situated on the Little River (figure 52). The primacy of farmers and artisans gave way to hourly workers, skilled laborers, and industrial machinery. Community elders and local business and religious leaders acquiesced to wealthy investors and company managers. Industrial timekeeping assumed new importance as men worked from whistle to whistle rather than from dawn to dusk. These changes altered how outsiders saw Tuckaleechee Cove. Maps, newspapers, and railroad schedules marked Townsend rather than the older but less precise geographic location of Tuckaleechee Cove. For many long-time residents, these changes must have seemed frightening and unsettling, while for others it meant increased opportunities and new challenges.[1]

Even before the creation of the Little River Lumber Company, the timber industry was an important part of the South's and Tuckaleechee Cove's economies. Many parts of the South had experienced sustained lumber booms as outside investors looked for tracts of virgin timber to harvest. Between 1877 and 1888, investors bought more than 5.7 million acres of southern woodland, and processed lumber flowed out of Florida, Mississippi, Arkansas, Louisiana, and Texas. New harvesting techniques and better transportation routes allowed large corporations to cut down centuries-old stands of virgin timber. When a United States

1. *Maryville Enterprise*, November 18, 1906.

Figure 52. Townsend Mill No. 2, which burned in 1916. (Hooks Collection, Great Smoky Mountains National Park, GRSM-32885.)

government report released information about millions of uncut acres in the mountains of North Carolina and Tennessee, lumber companies focused on those areas. Previously inaccessible because of rough terrain, mountains now lay open to companies with portable sawmills, railroad equipment, and an eager workforce. Investors bought available land and headed toward the southern Appalachians.[2]

The industrial development of Tuckaleechee Cove corresponded to the lumber boom that took place elsewhere in the South. The rapid growth of the Little River Lumber Company after 1901 proved to be economically beneficial to the area, and unlike in some hollows of West Virginia and Kentucky where industrialization sparked intense social unrest, the industry in Tuckaleechee Cove, with its new owners and imported labor, generally coexisted on friendly terms with the preexisting community. No labor conflicts apparently surfaced. Although feelings of trepidation no doubt existed among some in the cove before 1901, apprehension about new industry and newcomers seems not to have hindered industrial expansion.

2. C. Vann Woodward, *Origins of the New South* (Baton Rouge: Louisiana State University Press, 1951), 116–20.

In 1900 a group of investors from New York and Pennsylvania, including W. B. Townsend, toured Tuckaleechee and the surrounding area. Born and raised in Pennsylvania, Townsend (figure 53) had previously been a successful businessman with interests in lumber, coal, and railroads. In April 1901 he and a group of surveyors traveled around Tuckaleechee Cove examining property when heavy snow trapped them and local residents had to rescue them. Townsend had hoped to keep his intent a secret to minimize land speculation, but after his rescue he announced that he hoped to build three sawmills and a railroad line in Tuckaleechee Cove. The area had timber and enough water from the Little River to supply the needs of steam mills, mill ponds, and a growing population. Townsend moved to Tuckaleechee Cove to oversee the construction of company facilities and to set up the lumber operation.[3]

Although Tuckaleechee Cove had been home in the late 1800s to many individual loggers and small sawmills, nothing prepared its rural residents for rapid industrial development and the growth of a new town, Townsend, after 1902. Vast amounts of raw timber came down from the mountains and into Tuckaleechee Cove (figures 54 through 56). Over the course of its history, the Little River Lumber Company cut, milled, and shipped more than 560 million board feet of lumber. Much of the time the company operated its sawmills night and day to keep up with demand. The new industry required new buildings, most of it housing for new workers. The new railroad, first built from Maryville into the cove, reached the new

Figure 53. Colonel W. B. Townsend standing in the tracks of Little River Railroad in front of the General Office, Townsend, Tennessee. (Hooks Collection, Great Smoky Mountains National Park, III-L-17032, GRSM-32784.)

3. Blount County Charters, 1891–1941: 177–178, 193, in McClung Collection, Knox County Public Library, Knoxville, TN; *Maryville Times*, October 26, 1901.

Figure 54. Early days of the Little River Railroad in Townsend. (Vance Collection, Great Smoky Mountains National Park, II L-4179, GRSM-24006-bs.)

Figure 55. Little River Lumber Company steam shovel and log skidder (in background), dated after 1911 and probably before 1918. (Vance Collection, Great Smoky Mountains National Park, III-L-4178, GRSM-24006-bp.)

Figure 56. Little River Railroad Engine No. 110, Townsend, when the engine was new, probably about 1911–12. (Vance Collection, Great Smoky Mountains National Park, III-L-4183, GRSM-24006-bv.)

station at Townsend in September 1902. Soon new reports discussed a prospective eight additional miles to connect with Abrams Creek and more distant mountains.[4]

New railroad construction stimulated commercial growth. Though never fully isolated from the outside world, Tuckaleechee Cove became even more tightly integrated into national markets.

New businesses to serve the mill and its workers emerged after 1904. Entrepreneurs clustered their businesses near the offices and mills of the Little River Lumber Company in Townsend. One observer sensed change and noted that in general the area was enjoying "a boom, spelled with a big B, and we can safely predict great things for it in the future especially if the R.R. is continued to some of the coves or thickly wood districts near here." By late 1902 plans and contracts for forty new homes had been made public, and rumors that W. R. Swan, a major Pennsylvania investor in the lumber company, had been looking for a new house in the area, further stoked the public's excitement. Enthusiasm continued to grow after the completion of a new electric light plant and a large hotel in 1903. One breathless

4. Lambert, "Logging on Little River, 1890–1940," 35–36, 42; *Maryville Times*, May 15, 1905; Brown, *Wild East*, 54–55; Burns, *Blount County*, 231, 94, 260.

report from Tuckaleechee Cove warned that it would not be long until Townsend was one of the largest towns in the county: "They have a daily train and 'progress' is their watchword."[5]

More people required new governmental and cultural buildings. The newly constructed Townsend Inn offered comfortable accommodations for visitors, and a new post office replaced the old Tang post office that had been a social center in the cove. For a list of Tuckaleechee Cove and Townsend postmasters by date, see table 5. In 1902 a new high school was built, and it became the natural gathering point for the cove. In October 1903 the Blount County School Board held a teacher's institute at Townsend for teachers living in the area.[6]

TABLE 5. TUCKALEECHEE COVE AND TOWNSEND POST OFFICES AND POSTMASTERS, 1833–1962

Postmaster	Date	Postmaster	Date
George Snider	1/28/1833	Fredrick S. Emert	10/7/1893
James Matson	4/20/1838	Joseph W. Cameron	10/13/1897
George Freshour	10/4/1842	George B. Townsend	7/26/1902
George Snider	5/13/1856	Wilson B. Townsend	8/2/1905
William R. Snider	7/8/1872	Claude Dunn	2/13/1914
Samuel D. Langhram	8/27/1874	John C. Farmer	4/1/1921
Daniel H. Emert	6/22/1874	Dock H. Tipton	8/10/1921
Levi P. Dunn	12/19/1882	Marvie L. Tipton	12/11/1926
Frederick S. Emert	2/26/1886	Fred G. Ezell	5/23/1934
David A. Yearout	9/11/1889	John W. Dunn	6/22/1962

The arrival of the big lumber company and the railroad boosted the economic potential of nearby communities. In 1901 the Schlosser Leather Company of Walland opened a factory that processed more than three hundred hides a day. In 1903 that company advertised that it needed five thousand tons of chestnut and oak bark to maintain production. The firm was willing to pay $6.50 per ton for chestnut and oak, $5.00 per ton for hemlock, and $3.50 per ton for black oak; the only stipulation was that local "peelers" bring only good-quality bark in dry condition. A Maryville businessman opened a new mill and advertised that "all grades of poplar" would be bought anywhere along the Little River Railroad, and cash would be paid when loaded. Residents in Cades Cove, far up above Tuckaleechee, likewise understood the benefit of the railroad to ship their lumber to Maryville by way of Townsend.[7]

5. *Maryville Times*, December 22, 1900, August 9, September 6, November 15, 1902, February 21, 1903.

6. *Maryville Times*, October 3, 1903. See table 5 for a list of postmasters by date.

7. Burns, *History of Blount County*, 242; *Maryville Times*, March 21, April 11, 1903; Dunn, *Cades Cove*, 226.

Growing Pains

The frequency and severity of industrial mishaps increased as more men worked more dangerous jobs. Accidents were costly for the lumber company and railroad. When Jack McKenzie, a train engineer, missed a rail switch, he sent a trainload of lumber into a parked steam engine and took both engines out of service. Timber crews were subject to accidents as they cut and hauled timber from isolated spots (figures 57 and 58). In 1914 Andy Farmer,

Figure 57. Skid road with horses and J. pit. (Tipton Collection, Great Smoky Mountains National Park, GRSM-24018-m.)

Figure 58. Sherman Myers logging up Anthony Creek. (Hooks Collection, Great Smoky Mountains National Park, III-L-16576, GRSM-32825.)

a conductor on the Little River Railroad, was badly injured after falling from a train while trying to unload a railcar into the millpond in Townsend and two logs rolled over his body. Nothing, however, rivaled the destructive fires. In February 1906 a fast-moving fire destroyed the main mill building and two railroad cars before the sprinkler system doused the flames and saved the planing mill and administrative offices. The fire, believed to have started in the sawmill department, destroyed equipment and lumber valued at $50,000. W. B. Townsend noted that the company had only $20,000 in insurance on the building, but he was confident that the mill would be rebuilt. Another fire in 1916 consumed the main planing mill, sawmill, dry kiln, and ice plant of the lumber company, resulting in damage totaling $70,000.[8]

Violent fights were common in the lumber camps. In 1904 a gunfight broke out among drunken workers, and it left Walter Heffner dead from a bullet to the back. In 1906, when Ruben Bird, son of a prominent local merchant and an employee of the Little River Lumber Company, ordered five men to get to work, they responded with gunfire. When the shooting stopped, Bird lay mortally wounded. Sheriff's deputies eventually caught all five men.[9]

8. *Maryville Times*, May 19, 1905; February 23, 1906; June 29, 1916.

9. *Maryville Times*, August 28, 1914, August 23, 1906; *Maryville Record*, August 1904.

By the time of such alcohol-provoked violence, the issue of alcohol consumption was already controversial. For most of the 1800s, whiskey production provoked little opposition. Then, in the late 1880s, a temperance movement gained support in Blount County. Local newspapers condemned whiskey making. Led by the Temperance Alliance, the prohibition movement quickly became an important political force. The *Maryville Times* ran articles on the evils of alcohol. Editorials declared that temperance was gaining ground in Blount County; as one noted, "The time was when distilling whisky was considered a very respectable business and some of the most respected citizens engaged in it but now a whisky dealer of any kind is considered rather a questionable character." The copper kettles, tubing, and oak barrels of local still owners began to disappear or move to more remote locations in Tuckaleechee Cove. In 1887 Blount County voters approved by a margin of almost two to one an ordinance banning the sale of alcohol, but residents of Tuckaleechee Cove voted overwhelmingly against it, as did much of the rest of the state. But local temperance laws made stills illegal, and whiskey makers in Tuckaleechee Cove became targets of enforcement agents.[10]

Residents of the cove tried, however, to hold on to their traditional craft. In 1902 William Davis was arrested for operating a "wild cat" still on his property. The arrival of the Little River Lumber Company created a large, new demand for whiskey as lumber workers found a local supply among farmers. Company officials warned their employees and local distillers, now known as moonshiners, against buying and selling liquor in the lumber camps. In 1907 a company employee shot Black Jim Burchfield, who had ignored the warnings not to peddle whiskey in the camps. Company officials worried about retaliation from Burchfield's family after the shooter's charges were reduced from murder, but eventually the tension eased. The temperance movement finally gained majority support. In 1907 the city of Knoxville went "dry," and statewide prohibition was instituted in 1910. But that did not mean the end of whiskey making—or violence resulting from moonshining. In 1911 federal marshals destroyed a still known in cove legend as "Old Dad," which produced more than one hundred gallons per day. In 1919 Levi Patty confronted his brother-in-law Giles Hannah about stealing his still. Patty attacked Hannah with a pair of brass knuckles, and then Hannah shot and killed Patty, which prompted the sheriff to sweep through the cove destroying stills. Whiskey making in Tuckaleechee Cove was getting dangerous, and it slowly disappeared.[11]

Spring freshets and high water had once been essential to moving logs down the Little River, but flooding in Tuckaleechee Cove's industrial period mostly brought unwelcome destruction. With large, expensive sawmills along the river and company offices on the floodplain, flooding caused confusion and delay. In November 1906 torrents of water rushed through the Little River valley, destroying miles of railroad track and stranding timber cars

10. *Maryville Republican*, December 6, 1873; *Maryville Times*, March 15, 1907, February 3 and 24, 1886, October 5, 1887, June 21, 1902, June 2, 1905.

11. *Maryville Times*, February 24, 1911, June 7, 1907, January 7, 1920; *Maryville Post*, December 31, 1919.

in the mountains above Townsend. Flooding also destroyed local milldams and halted flour production in Tuckaleechee Cove until repairs could be made.[12]

Such setbacks hardly slowed the new growth in Tuckaleechee Cove. In 1900, in the place that became Townsend, there were two general stores, two blacksmith forges, a flour mill, a sawmill, and a post office. Six years later the town had two physicians, four general stores, two lumber companies, a hotel, a railroad station, and a variety of other small businesses. Better roads allowed rural residents to spend money easily not just in Townsend but also in Maryville, Sevierville, and Knoxville. But it was the railroad that truly expanded the geographic bounds of the people of the cove. Residents could take an early train to Maryville and then connect to Knoxville aboard the Knoxville and Augusta Railroad. The trip from Maryville to Knoxville took an hour and cost fifty cents. From Knoxville, travelers could take the No. 1 to Harriman, Tennessee, then on to Lexington, Kentucky, and finally to Cincinnati, Ohio. Or they could take the No. 3 to Coal Creek and Jellico, Tennessee, or the No. 12 to Morristown, Tennessee, then to Asheville, North Carolina, and on to points farther east. A person leaving Tuckaleechee in the morning could be in Kentucky, Virginia, North Carolina, Georgia, or Alabama by late afternoon.[13]

Life in a Growing Community

Despite the rapid growth of Tuckaleechee Cove during the first decade of the 1900s, many aspects of rural life remained as they had been for the past century. Daily habits remained relatively untouched. Farm life revolved around natural rhythms and changed little after the intrusion of nearby industry. As the winter of 1903 turned into the spring of 1904, residents of Tuckaleechee Cove prepared for the upcoming planting season. Farmers and gardeners fretted over fields of corn and wheat and rows of peas as heavy rains delayed work. Despite too much rain, however, local residents managed to plant their crops, and as the winter wheat ripened, news of the new "little Columbia" threshing machine circulated around Tuckaleechee Cove. Nor did the wet weather stop the Little River Lumber Company. Logging crews continued to cut timber, and the mills in Townsend managed to stay open despite the threat of flooding. Local independent loggers S. R. Law and George Brickey continued to log their land with crosscut saws and axes and drag timber to nearby mills with mules and chains. Railroad workers labored through the rain and mud to complete the new spur up the mountain to Cades Cove. Residents of Tuckaleechee Cove knew that the locomotive would forever change the stillness of Cades Cove, as it had their home.[14]

---

12. *Maryville Enterprise*, November 22, 1906.

13. *Young and Co.'s Business and Professional Directory of the Cities and Towns of Tennessee.* (Atlanta, GA: Young & Company, 1907), 490, 251–53, 472–73; *Maryville Times* August 10, 1901.

14. *Maryville Record*, August 5, 1904.

In 1906 a reporter arriving in Townsend found a vibrant mixture of old and new. He heard the "hum of push and energy" and saw cozy new cottages that housed "happy and prosperous employees of the saw mill." From an outsider's perspective, the whole town had assumed the "tireless energy and indomitable will" of W. B. Townsend. The reporter watched in awe as "great burly logs which looked to us unfit for lumber were, by a few rips of the saw, shaped into comely timbers, fit for the builder's use." He ventured out into the countryside where he met John Myers, a well-to-do farmer, and William Dunn, a young merchant "who is growing in favor and in business." W. T. Lawson milled wheat into flour "to feed the thrifty denizens of the cove." The reporter also ran into Dr. L. J. Jenkins who had a "nice house on the pinnacle of a miniature mountain from which he can overlook the beautiful valley around him." After a full day of walking around Tuckaleechee Cove, the reporter had dinner at Henry Webb's house, where he enjoyed a full meal of "delicious mountain honey and hot biscuits, to which you may add the best of butter and milk."[15]

Residents found their traditional entertainments, social interactions, and business dealings enhanced by the greater mobility the railroad offered. In 1904 twenty-three revelers from Tuckaleechee Cove took two rail cars from Townsend to an "Egg Boiling and Ice Cream Supper" in Walland to support the Epworth League of the Methodist Episcopal Church. Friends and family constantly visited each other and took time to visit Maryville, Knoxville, and places far from East Tennessee. W. B. Townsend took extended trips to New York, Pennsylvania, and Atlanta. Good rail connections allowed William Abbott to come home from college in Chicago for Christmas break. Peddlers took advantage of Tuckaleechee Cove's new railroad and roamed the area selling goods at "scandalously low prices." Representatives of the Chicago Portrait Company set up a temporary photographic studio in Townsend and began taking pictures of local citizens for a fee.[16]

As his timber crews and railroad laborers pushed farther into the mountains, W. B. Townsend became the area's greatest philanthropist. He helped finance the construction of a new high school in 1905 and continued to aid local schools by holding fundraisers. His support for a new church prompted its being named for his wife: the Margaret Townsend Memorial Methodist Church. Margaret Townsend also founded the Ladies Aid Society, which helped fund local schools and provided assistance to small mountain churches. She made Christmas gifts to needy children and adults each year.[17]

The Impact of Industry on the Tuckaleechee Environment

The Little River Lumber Company brought drastic environmental change as it harvested thousands of acres of hardwood forests in eastern Tennessee and western North Carolina.

15. *Maryville Enterprise*, October 18, 1906.

16. *Maryville Record*, April 8, December 22, 1904.

17. *Maryville Times*, August 12, 1919, February 25, March 4, 1926.

Railroad engines belched smoke and cinders into the air, and whirling saws spewed dust. Loggers pushed deep into the Smoky Mountains, using new techniques to extract timber from deep ravines and steep slopes. Their new technology included ground skidders, overhead cable systems, and incline railroads. In 1924 company officials estimated that a new railroad track into previously untouched forest would yield ten years' worth of timber for the company. The Little River Lumber Company cut entire forests of ash, basswood, birch, buckeye, cherry, hemlock, maple, poplar, oak, and spruce. In about two decades, the firm was one of eight large lumber companies in the region that denuded a significant portion of the Smoky Mountains. W. B. Townsend was thus one of several exploitative capitalists who wreaked havoc in the mountains. But he was aware of the environmental impact of his company's actions and made some effort to promote scientific forestry and government forestry reserves. He apparently always intended, after he had harvested the timber, to give his mountain land to the United States Forest Service to be replanted and rejuvenated under federal control. Townsend did preserve the forest around Elkmont, an old lumber camp converted to a mountain resort, as a destination for tourists.[18]

Large profits and good jobs caused some residents of the cove to look the other way from the ecological destruction created by the timber harvests. In 1915 the *Maryville Times* warned Blount County residents about the risks of environmental damage in an article headlined "Keep The Streams Clean and Pure." Instead of chastising local industry, however, the article reminded picnickers to pick up their trash near springs, rivers, and lakes that might contribute "to your day's pleasure." It further warned fishermen to clean their catch away from the water and suggested that farmers divert their barnyard waste away from streams.[19]

To residents of the cove, perhaps the most obvious environmental impact was the sudden creation of a busy town. The overall population of the district doubled between 1890 and 1910. In 1908 there were seventy-one births and nine deaths there, a ratio that meant mushrooming population growth. All harvested trees eventually ended up in the millponds and yards in Townsend before being shipped out on the Little River Railroad. During the flush years of the 1920s, Townsend's mills cut on average 22 million board feet per year. The company built steam-powered band saws, planing mills, drying racks, holding ponds, a power plant, a machine shop, and administrative offices in Townsend. It constructed scores of houses for workers. In 1930, 183 of 382, or 48 percent, of the heads of households in Tuckaleechee Cove worked for the lumber company or the railroad. When the steam whistle blew at Townsend in the morning, a variety of men went to work: forty forest laborers, fifty-three mill laborers, twenty-two lumber yard workers, and eleven railroad laborers,

18. *Maryville Times*, November 3, 1924; Brown, *Wild East*, 54–55, 58; Christopher B. Martin, "Selling the Southern Highlands: Tourism and Community Development in the Mountain South" (PhD diss., University of Tennessee), 123; Vic Weals, *Last Train to Elkmont: A Look Back at Life on Little River in the Great Smoky Mountains* (Knoxville, TN: Olden Press, 1993), 9–16.

19. *Maryville Times*, November 11, 1915.

as well as workers in other occupations ranging from the president of the company to the man who sharpened the saw blades.

Shifting Lifestyles

Improved roads made movement in, out, and through Tuckaleechee much faster and more common. In 1901 support for better roads led to the creation of the East Tennessee Good Roads Association, which became the state highway commission and is today the Tennessee Department of Transportation (TDOT). In 1915 Blount County commissioners approved $300,000 for a new road from Tuckaleechee to Cades Cove. The road became an important link for tourists. By 1919 Tuckaleechee Cove had 12.4 miles of paved roads, replacing many of the old dirt surfaces that had been a part of rural life since the beginning of EuroAmerican settlement.[20]

New roads enabled progress in education. They made it possible for rural school districts to meet for an all-day, in-service workshop, and the county government approved funding for traveling libraries to enter the area so that "lovers of books and literature [could] get the best books without cost." Schools fostered a general sense of development and pride in Tuckaleechee Cove and became main centers of community life in the way that churches had been in the early nineteenth century. In 1919 the county school system matched the $1,500 donated by W. B. Townsend for a new school in Townsend. The company president also agreed to pay the principal's salary for the first school year. Now the cove had eight schools, most of them one-room primaries. Outside the classroom, schools began offering more services, and teachers assumed new roles in the community. Malinda King, a teacher at Red Bank, organized a literary society for the benefit of her students and the community. Schools sponsored social events to raise money. In 1919 the Townsend Grammar School held an "old-fashioned pie supper." In 1925 a group of local boys and girls met at the high school and organized scout troops. As the largest public building in Tuckaleechee Cove, Townsend High School also became a popular meeting place for large groups. The newly formed Parents and Teachers Association hosted a "Father's Night" program at the school that highlighted the role of the father in the life and education of young children. Students from Townsend Elementary held a public recital that included singing, dancing, music, comedy skits, and a flower pageant. Performers from Townsend High staged annual plays such as "A Rustic Romeo," a romantic comedy, and "The Mummy and the Mumps" for the community.[21]

20. *Maryville Times*, August 20, 1909; October 14, 1915; April 9, 1919; Dunn, *Cades Cove*, 224; Ronald G. Schmidt and William S. Hooks, *Whistle Over the Mountain: Timber, Track, and Trails in the Tennessee Smokies* (Yellow Springs, OH: Graphicom Press, 1994).

21. *Maryville Times*, October 15, November 19, 1919, September 22, 1924, February 26, 1925.

Social life in the cove now often took place in fraternal and agricultural organizations. The Odd Fellows fraternal group built a hall in Townsend where they held yearly celebrations and picnics for the community. There were usually not more than fifteen Odd Fellows at a time, but they were active. By 1920 men in Townsend had also formed a Masonic lodge. In 1915 twenty Tuckaleechee Cove farmers organized a Farmers' Alliance to promote scientific methods in agriculture, including maintaining experimental fields, and to operate a cooperative store in Townsend.[22]

Farming held a less important place in the economic order of the twentieth century, and it was undergoing fundamental changes in animal husbandry. Before the early twentieth century, livestock freely foraged in woods and fields. The burden of protecting gardens, haystacks, crops, and farmyards belonged to the landowner, not the one with title to the livestock. Fences were built to keep cattle and hogs out, not to keep livestock in. Hogs fed on chestnuts and acorns, and cows and horses grazed on wild grasses and leaves. But this easy and inexpensive means to feed livestock also resulted in destruction by wandering animals. A new state stock law in 1907 required farmers to keep cattle, sheep, goats, and swine penned, and livestock owners were liable for damage done to personal property by loose livestock. Farmers had to build fences in response to the law, typically using split rails to create "worm" or "snake" fences. This change angered small farmers who had relied on free range to feed their livestock.[23]

Whereas nineteenth-century residents of Tuckaleechee Cove looked to their churches as their primary social outlets, twentieth-century inhabitants began integrating school, work, sports, and other activities into their social lives. School team sports created pride among cove residents. Baseball games played in Townsend at the high school became community social events. A newspaper reported in 1921 that a close game between Townsend and Maryville was one of the best contests ever played at the Townsend ballpark. In 1931 Townsend opened a school gymnasium that not only the Townsend community but also, as the *Maryville Times* reported, "the entire county may be proud of." Soon boys' and girls' basketball teams ran up and down the hardwood court with a "T" stitched to their uniforms.[24]

Religion remained a vibrant part of life in Tuckaleechee Cove. Churches still served as spiritual and social centers for many residents, even if other institutions now filled many social and communal needs. Older congregations took advantage of the influx of new people and began holding large, well-publicized revivals. In 1901 Tuckaleechee Chapel proselytized among new timber workers, and in 1915 Reverend Dykes of Bethel Church baptized thirty-four people on one autumn evening. As cars and the railroad further opened Tuckaleechee Cove to outsiders,

---

22. *Maryville Times*, May 25, 1902, October 26, 1906, January 7, 1920, October 28, 1915; Maryville College, *Social Survey of Blount County* (Maryville, TN, 1930).

23. *Maryville Times*, April 19, 1907, July 2, 1919; Wilma Dykeman and Jim Stokely, *Highland Homeland: The People of the Great Smokies* (Washington, DC: National Park Service, Division of Publications, 1978), 19–23.

24. *Maryville Times*, November 11, 1921, February 5, 1931.

larger revivals were held. In the fall of 1919, Tuckaleechee Chapel invited people to visit "an old fashion get-together meeting . . . Bring your lunch and spend the day with us and let's have a real good happy day." After three weeks of revival, almost one hundred souls were converted. Seven years later, another large revival attracted even larger crowds to the Margaret Townsend Memorial Methodist Church to hear traveling preachers and guest speakers.[25]

Outsiders Find Tuckaleechee Cove

By the end of the 1920s the logging and milling operations based in Tuckaleechee Cove had peaked. Large forests had been clear-cut. The potential for higher profits had waned, and W. B. Townsend began to wonder openly about the future of his mountain investments. He believed it was not economically feasible for him to reforest the region and wait for a second generation of trees to mature. There was no other market for the cutover land. The end of the Little River Lumber Company meant an even greater change in lifestyle for Townsend's workers. The demise of the lumber company meant unemployment and hardship.[26]

Then the Great Depression of the 1930s devastated the demand for new building materials and depressed the production of the Little River Lumber Company to less than 2 million board feet of lumber per year. Saws and train engines fell silent. Over the 1930s decade, less than forty years after entering the region, the Little River Lumber Company and most of its equipment disappeared, and within a few years, the once-thriving town of Townsend became a quaint collection of homes nestled along the banks of the Little River, with little to remind a visitor that it had once been a vibrant industrial village. By 1939 Tuckaleechee Cove's industrial period faded into history as shrinking forests and poor lumber markets forced the closure of the Little River Lumber Company. As the last logs rolled away from company sawmills, a local observer noted that Townsend, long the center of industry in Blount County, was now only a residential town. Soon the lumber company, which at times had employed over five hundred workers, would be "a matter of history." The Little River Railroad, once a source of local excitement and pride, closed, and much of its track was pulled up. Between 1941 and 1944, much of the equipment and buildings owned by the lumber company and railroad was disposed of as salvage. A strange new silence settled over the small community.[27]

A Void Filled

Tourism had long been a minor feature of the Tuckaleechee Cove economy. For people in an increasingly urbanized and industrialized nation, the small towns and mountains of

25. *Maryville Times*, December 6, 1901, September 23, 1919.

26. Lambert, "Logging on Little River, 1890–1940," 38–41.

27. *Maryville Times*, October 25 and 26, 1939.

eastern Tennessee seemed different enough to enjoy as a vacation spot. In 1832 the Montvale Springs Hotel and Resort had opened at the western end of the cove as a summer mountain refuge for southerners. Guests spent days hunting, fishing, socializing, and eating. Montvale Springs remained popular until the Civil War interrupted business. After years of neglect and poor management, it reopened in 1902 as a resort for middle-class travelers. New railroad connections and roads enabled vacationers to enjoy the mountain air and water of the Great Smoky Mountains. In 1906 a visitor to Tuckaleechee Cove observed the mountain streams "of limpid clearness . . . massive rocks and precipitous mountains while the river's alternate eddy and plunge give it a peculiar beauty and attractiveness." In the meantime, area residents had built cottages along the western border of Tuckaleechee Cove at Kinzel Springs. Begun in 1894, the Kinzel Springs resort grew with the arrival of the railroad. In 1911 twenty workmen from Knoxville built a resort so that more tourists could enjoy the good mountain air. Some Tuckaleechee Cove residents became well known to tourists looking for a taste of local color. William Walker, dressed in homespun cloth and seemingly a product of another era, sold honey, baskets, barrels, fruit, and furs to visitors. His reputation as a local character spread, and visitors came to meet Walker, to see him leap upward and click his heels and tell hunting stories.[28]

Even while the timber industry thrived, Tuckaleechee Cove had remained popular with tourists looking for rural retreats and mountain getaways. New ambitions for a tourist trade emerged in the 1920s. In 1926 plans were proposed for a large summer resort in the cove, one that would include a manmade lake, a golf course, and other amenities on 1,300 acres of land. Later the lumber company offered land to anyone willing to open a hotel in Townsend. All these efforts to rejuvenate tourism in Tuckaleechee Cove finally foundered with the Great Depression.[29]

As industrial profits dwindled during the late 1920s and early 1930s, interest in a national park in the Smoky Mountains increased among landowners, politicians, philanthropists, and the public. By 1926 there were reported to be several campaigns for a "Great Smoky Mountains National Park." David Chapman, a Knoxville businessman, led an effort to purchase much of the remaining virgin forests. Blount County residents raised $12,000 to help establish the park, despite some concern that increased governmental control might undermine property-owner rights through use of eminent domain. A local newspaper editor worried that Blount County would be "robbed of taxes, of highways, and other features necessary for the county's growth." Others speculated that the mountain park might take control of towns like Townsend. But despite the numerous misgivings, men with political influence in Nashville and Washington, D.C., worked to get state and national support

28. Martin, "Selling of the Southern Highlands," 25–26, 58; *Maryville Enterprise*, October 18, 1906; *Maryville Times*, February 17, 1911, September 13, 1912; Weals, *Last Train to Elkmont*, 9–16.

29. *Maryville Post*, August 3, 1926; *Maryville Times*, March 15, 1928, October 26, 1939.

for the park. In June 1934 the efforts came to fruition when the Great Smoky Mountains National Park was opened to visitors.[30]

Soon Tuckaleechee Cove was filled with visitors on their way to the new park. Drawn by grand mountain vistas, waterfalls, and challenging hiking trails, tourists used Townsend as a gateway to the Smokies, and local businessmen began catering to tourist needs. The vast expansion of automobile ownership by the 1930s and 1940s made it easier to pass by the farms and fields of Tuckaleechee Cove in search of the majesty of Clingmans Dome, Mount LeConte, and Cades Cove. As early as 1939, the Great Smoky Mountains National Park reported that in one month 13,175 visitors in 4,620 cars entered the park from forty states. Tuckaleechee Cove had become less a separate, unique place and was now encompassed as part of the new national park.

Suggested Readings

Brown, Margaret L. *The Wild East: A Biography of the Great Smoky Mountains*. Gainesville: University Press of Florida, 2000. A good account of the larger region around Tuckaleechee Cove.

Dunn, Durwood. *Cades Cove: The Life and Death of a Southern Appalachian Community, 1818–1937*. Knoxville: University of Tennessee Press, 1988. Provides interesting detail on the twentieth-century changes in the region.

Dykeman, Wilma, and Jim Stokely. *Highland Homeland: The People of the Great Smokies*. Washington, DC: National Park Service, Division of Publications, 1978. An affectionate account of the mountain people.

Pierce, Daniel S. *The Great Smokies: From Natural Habitat to National Park*. Knoxville: University of Tennessee Press, 2000. The best source for information on the creation of the Great Smoky Mountains National Park.

30. Daniel S. Pierce, *The Great Smokies: From Natural Habitat to National Park* (Knoxville: University of Tennessee Press, 2000), 113–14; *Maryville Times*, February 15 and 25, 1926, April 14 and 18, 1927.

Chapter 7

NEW DEVELOPMENTS IN TUCKALEECHEE COVE

But the story of the Tuckaleechee Cove is not finished. The present is the history of tomorrow. This chapter briefly explores new developments in Tuckaleechee Cove, summarizes its human history with an emphasis on trends through time, and concludes with a note about its future.

Heritage Tourism in Tuckaleechee Cove

While a rural area even today, Tuckaleechee Cove has always been an important entity in the regional economy, importing resources from outside and exporting resources from the cove. Even from ancient times, communication lanes and transportation routes (figure 59) have been at the center of these interactions. While this book has told the story of many human groups that looked upon, and changed for better or worse, the face of Tuckaleechee Cove, our story would not be complete without mention of another important actor, the Tennessee Department of Transportation (TDOT). As it has done with so many other areas of the state, TDOT has profoundly affected the cove in recent years; its impact continues today and will continue to pay dividends into the future. Following its charge to provide for public transportation and promote economic prosperity for citizens of Tennessee and its visitors, TDOT undertook to create a more easily accessible gateway to the Smokies by widening the highway (US 321) into the cove from Maryville. In the process, which began officially on June 11, 1999, with letting of a construction contract, easy access has resulted in increased numbers of visitors to the cove and Great Smoky Mountains National Park. Nearly 20 million people visit the park each year; many of these visitors enjoy the easy access provided through Tuckaleechee Cove.

But as previous chapters noted, important archaeological remains were found in the path of the new highway. As part of the process of developing or revamping any Tennessee state road or federal highway, TDOT, often in conjunction with the Federal Highway

Figure 59. The Great Smoky Mountains Heritage Center in Townsend exhibits a large collection of historic horse-drawn wagons and buggies to tell the story of transportation in Tuckaleechee Cove.

Administration, follows a process of evaluation of the likely consequences of proposed highway changes. Among many other categories, cultural resources are considered. To find archaeological and historic resources, archaeologists perform a survey like those in the 1990s that identified the archaeological remains explored as part of the widening of US Highway 321. Once important resources that will be disturbed or destroyed by construction are identified, a program is designed to lessen the impact of the project on these resources.

Development of the program included consultation with groups that had a vested interest or stake in the project. One such group was the Eastern Band of Cherokee Indians, a Native American group from in and around Cherokee, North Carolina. Others involved in discussions and concurrence included the Tennessee Division of Archaeology, the Tennessee State Historic Preservation Officer, the Tennessee Commission on Indian Affairs, and the Chickasaw Nation. Other Native American organizations with connections to the southern Appalachian area were invited to review plans; some chose to designate their representation to the Eastern Band of Cherokee Indians.

An official agreement (a legal document called a Memorandum of Agreement) was worked out and first signed in April 2001 and amended in the fall of 2003 that outlined and itemized the steps to be undertaken by each party to insure that cultural resources were properly treated and that interests of the public and the various stakeholders were satisfied. The memorandum called for investigation of the archaeological and historical resources within the project, and included provisions calling for walking paths along the new highway with a set of informative signs explaining the archaeological finds that were retrieved during construction. Also, a public exhibit of the archaeological materials recovered from the Big Dig was authorized and funded.

This exhibit was originally slated by the Memorandum of Agreement for the Visitor's Center in Townsend, but some individuals in the local community united to form a committee with a loftier vision: creation of a freestanding heritage center. Thus was born the Great Smoky Mountains Heritage Center, portrayed in figure 60, supported by a combination of private and public funds. During construction, the archaeologists from TDOT and the University of Tennessee worked with the newly hired staff from the Heritage Center to plan exhibits. Some of the artifacts from the Big Dig were placed on exhibit, and residents of the community loaned many other artifacts, particularly historic tools and implements, to the Heritage Center.

Construction for the Heritage Center began in June of 2002; its grand opening was held on the evening of February 6, 2006. Over 2,000 guests attended. Since that time, the center

Figure 60. The Great Smoky Mountains Heritage Center is open to the public and hosts about 29,000 visitors a year, many of whom are school-age children from the surrounding area. (Courtesy of the Great Smoky Mountains Heritage Center.)

has attracted nearly 250,000 visitors. In addition to tourists who visit the center and Tuckaleechee Cove, the Heritage Center provides an educational outreach to school groups from surrounding counties. Attendance has averaged about 7,900 school children a year since its opening. In addition to providing archaeological and historical exhibits within the building, the center offers outdoor exhibits of buildings, cabins, and barns, along with a covered amphitheater for festivals and concerts.

The outdoor exhibit area features buildings, such as the barn pictured in figure 61. Artifacts on display include numerous examples of old machinery, a small sawmill, and a famous moonshine still, all artifacts from the local area. A log cabin containing period furnishings (figure 62) allows visitors to explore and try out an old-fashioned bed or sit in an old rocking chair.

Another building is an example of the first "mobile home," a house that harks back to the days of the railroad. This small structure (figure 63), called a "setoff house," was built to be loaded onto a flatbed railroad car and transported to locations where nearby timber crews felled the grand trees of the Smokies or where railroad crews worked on the tracks or bed. The house was fully equipped as a temporary residence for a worker's family.

The impact of TDOT's emphasis and support of historic preservation and heritage tourism in Tuckaleechee Cove cannot be overstated. While the improvements to US Highway 321 were indeed expensive and the careful investigation of archaeological and historical resources quite time consuming, the result will serve the public interest for decades to come.

The Human History of the Cove

Human beings have had a profound influence on the ecological history of Tuckaleechee Cove, and likewise, the natural environment has affected human history. Native American foragers, aboriginal farmers, Cherokee refugees, EuroAmerican settlers, antebellum farmers and artisans, soldiers, industrialists, and, most recently, tourists have had different spatial relationships with the streams, fields, and forests of Tuckaleechee Cove, an area of about 265 square miles nestled in the western edge of the southern Appalachian Mountains of modern-day Tennessee. Each human group used the land differently; each applied newer and different technologies to exploit its resources. In exchange, the natural terrain influenced personal habits, housing construction, subsistence practices, technological innovations, and transportation routes for those living in the area.

Long before any human face saw Tuckaleechee Cove, tens of thousands of acres of gently rolling terrain supported lush floral and faunal communities. Floral communities were dominated by a mixed mesophysic forest canopy composed of red oak, post oak, white oak, chestnut oak, American chestnut, American beech, black walnut, sugar maple, silver maple, eastern hemlock, northern white cedar, eastern red cedar, basswood, tulip poplar, white ash, cucumber magnolia, black gum, sweet buckeye, and yellow buckeye. The herbaceous understory included members of the orchid family, rhododendrons, azaleas, redbud, pignut hickory, shagbark hickory, scarlet oak, dogwood, sourwood, American holly, sweetgum, spicebush, sassafras, butterfly weed, rattlesnake weed, sweetpepper bush, devil's walkingstick, poison ivy, wild blueberry, and blackberries.

Figure 61. Numerous old buildings and tools, mostly from the area, give the visitor to the Heritage Center a taste of life and work in rural Tuckaleechee Cove during the last two centuries.

Figure 62. Visitors to the Heritage Center can get the feel of life in the olden days from hands-on exhibits like this furnished cabin.

Figure 63. The "setoff house" (interior *above,* exterior *below*) was a practical solution to the housing shortage in temporary logging areas or railway construction sites.

These diverse flora supported varied fauna dominated by several large mammals including elk and white-tailed deer, black bear, and mountain lion (or cougar). Bison roamed as far east as the cove during late prehistory. Coyotes have an ancient pedigree in the East and were likely present in the cove for most of prehistory. Foxes, beavers, eastern cottontail rabbits, woodchucks, skunks, minks, mice, bats, and weasels are a few of the many medium- and small-sized mammals in the cove. Numerous amphibians and reptiles add to the diversity of the animal community, and the water courses within the cove attracted a large array of aquatic species including fish (gar, trout, bass, catfish) and aquatic birds such as wood ducks, mallards, and Canada geese. Eagles and turkeys were also common in the cove.

The Little River, perhaps the area's most prominent natural feature, has greatly influenced those who lived, traveled, and worked in its midst. Native Americans used the river as a navigational guide, and, no doubt, aquatic and other animal and plant resources provided an important focus of subsistence throughout human existence in the cove. The river cut through and exposed rock in its bed and within its banks that was of great utility to the earliest visitors to the cove. While most of the flint for sharp cutting tools fashioned by the first Tuckaleechee Cove residents was to be found in the best quality downstream from the cove, various sedimentary and igneous cobbles were sought out to serve for grinding, pounding, and chopping chores and as raw material for fashioning ornaments.

Early EuroAmerican settlers followed the river into Tuckaleechee Cove and settled on rich bottomland nourished by flooding. Nineteenth-century farmers, millers, tanners, coopers, and blacksmiths settled along the river and used its water as a source of power and supply. During the Civil War, the river provided forage for warring armies, and after the war the tributary became a natural waterway for loggers who floated timber to waiting mills. The Little River gave the lumber industry needed water for mill ponds, steam engines, and human consumption, and the river valley became a natural route for railroad construction. Tourists eventually came to enjoy its cool water and bountiful fishing opportunities. Tourism in Tuckaleechee Cove became especially important after the lumber industry began to wane, and unlike many rural areas in the South, Tuckaleechee Cove managed to remain economically and socially relevant after the departure of heavy industry.

From the earliest people to enter and occupy these rolling hills and valley, the natural resources of Tuckaleechee Cove have had different meanings to different human groups. For the first Native American foragers, entering the cove ten to twelve millennia ago, the biotic environment was perhaps most important, providing a virtual treasure trove of food resources for the taking. Foragers, those people who made a living through collecting of wild resources and hunting, depended on their keen knowledge of biotic resources: the timing of seed, fruit, and nut production in the cove's forests and the habits of food animals, particularly deer, bear, turkey, and squirrel. While archaeologists often imagine that these early settlers strategically stalked the animals, like elk, deer, or bear that provided large packages of meat protein, in practical terms these and some other prey animals often feed on some of the same seeds, nuts, and fruits sought out by humans. This factor suggests the real possibility that hunting of these game animals was often an activity imbedded in collecting, rather than the reverse. After all, careful scheduling to collect foods such as hickory nuts or acorns before other animals ate these nuts must have been a high priority.

Even as populations of foragers over eight or nine millennia began to more densely fill the landscape, foragers left a very light impact on the landscape and its resources compared to others who were to follow. It is not entirely clear when the people of the cove and East Tennessee in general began to turn to food production (plant tending or horticulture) as a strategy for subsistence. It was no doubt a gradual transition, perhaps somewhat experimental in nature. The starchy and oily plants first domesticated by foragers in the eastern Woodlands (see the first section of chapter 2) were precisely the weedy plants that are common to disturbed ground, ground like that near campsites that were used time and time again. Paleoethnobotanists can detect subtle changes to carbonized seeds that indicate domestication by about three millennia ago. This was the case with remains from the Big Dig. The trajectory towards food production culminated during the Mississippian period (about a thousand years ago) with adoption and use of crops such as corn and beans, plants originally domesticated in Mesoamerica, alongside other locally domesticated plants. Both Mississippian peoples and Cherokees who resided in the cove were farmers but unlike farmers of the historic period.

Native American farmers in the cove, both Mississippian peoples and Cherokees, relied for about half or maybe a bit more of their subsistence on food production. In both cases, agricultural fields were small, somewhat like a large garden. Bear in mind that clearing trees for agricultural fields in Tuckaleechee Cove would have been a formidable task using stone axes. Archaeologists think that trees were not actually chopped down in most cases but left standing after a process called girdling in which a sharp stone tool, a stone axe or chopper, was used to penetrate and groove the bark of the tree around its circumference, thereby killing the tree. Without foliage during the next growing season, enough sunlight would penetrate to allow crop growth. Crude chipped stone hoes (see figure 28) and sharply pointed digging sticks constituted the primary farming tools.

As described in chapters 2 and 3, the late prehistoric people living in the area of the Big Dig (the Mississippian peoples and the Cherokees) were distributed primarily in farmsteads or farm-related compounds consisting of a few buildings and the immediate area around them. While the town of Skittletown was apparently an exception, other Mississippian houses seem to have been associated with fenced or palisaded compounds. Were the agricultural fields (gardens) of the Mississippian occupants of the areas excavated at the Big Dig primarily within the bounds of the compounds? It is difficult to know the intent of late prehistoric and protohistoric gardening, but it is certain that Native American farmers of Tuckaleechee Cove left a light impact on the landscape compared to later, EuroAmerican inhabitants.

The economic scope of Tuckaleechee Cove changed as European-American farmers settled, cleared the land, developed the region, and made the land work for them. Native Americans had hunted in the forests and used the Little River as a natural transportation route but did low-impact farming by comparison to later farmers. Early EuroAmerican settlers cleared small patches of land to raise crops and livestock while the next generation of farmers expanded agricultural production by clearing additional land and using better farming methods. The steel plow pulled by horses, mules, or oxen allowed farmers to clear large continuous parcels of land, and of course, unexpected rains and floods routinely eroded and deflated newly plowed fields. More than a hundred years of poor agricultural practices across the South led to poor agricultural productivity prior to modern farming practices.

The soul of the cove was torn apart as war between the North and South placed it squarely in the sights of both armies. Civil War soldiers recognized the age-old natural passage that Tuckaleechee Cove provided between the east and west and used it as a byway during campaigns. As the wounds of war heeled, Tuckaleechee Cove returned to peaceful agrarian pursuits, but soon industrialists saw profit in the large, virgin forests that surrounded the cove. Shortly after the turn of the twentieth century, timbering rapidly removed the virgin forests of the surrounding mountains. As large-scale logging and milling in Tuckaleechee Cove faded by the late 1930s, the forces of nature rapidly reclaimed areas altered by human activity and renourished the land for the next generation of inhabitants.

Now, tourists enjoy the tranquil beauty of the rural community. Despite these differences and the changes each group made to the environment, Tuckaleechee Cove seemingly remains timeless in its splendor. Although stone axes, plows, saws, and dams temporarily altered the landscape, the region maintained its natural beauty and productivity. Fields continued to produce, forests continued to grow, and the Little River continued to flow despite the passing of successive human faces and time.

The Big Dig provided professional archaeologists with the first information on the prehistory of Tuckaleechee Cove. Likewise, the project devoted considerable time to investigating and compiling the local history of the cove. Together, these studies offered the first insight into the long history of the peoples of the cove.

The many faces of Tuckaleechee Cove saw amazing innovations in aspects of life, from technology and shelter to belief systems. These cultural changes can be likened to a snowball rolling down a hill, escalating in speed and increasing in size. The first people to enter the cove were foragers, organized into small, communal family bands, who subsisted on the abundant wild floral and faunal resources of the area. Even some ten or twelve millennia ago, these people were experts at making weapons and tools necessary to their lifestyle. Theories about the origins of the First Americans vary, so archaeologists do not yet know where, in general terms, these early people (that is, Paleoindians) came from, or if they used the atlatl as a weapon, but it is clear that they were experts in understanding the nature of their environment and its resources. There is no evidence from the Big Dig about provisions for shelter for these earliest foragers. Although spear or atlatl projectile points were recovered from the sites, it is not even clear that their users actually lived or camped in the vicinity of the sites.

Innovations in weaponry included the atlatl, or throwing stick, to assist the spear, and the bow and arrow, a weapon that came into the region about 1,400 or 1,500 years ago. Both the atlatl and the bow and arrow revolutionized hunting practices in their time, as did the firearm and the first deer rifles. There is not much archaeological evidence that the Cherokees of Tuckaleechee Cove possessed firearms. Two gunflints from flintlock rifles were found in a pit at the Big Dig, but only a single piece of iron (function unknown) was recovered. However, in general, rifles in the hands of Native Americans, including Cherokees, vastly increased the predation of white-tailed deer in the South, providing deerskins for trade to European markets. The deerskin trade was so pervasive in many communities that it destabilized the traditional economies of many Native American groups in the eastern woodlands.

Innovation in cooking technology included replacement of the hot-rock boiling technique with, first, stone (steatite and sandstone) bowls that could be heated directly over the fire and, later, with ceramic pots, properly fired to become impervious to liquids. Metal containers of course replaced these older cooking vessels, but many of the dishes on the southern US table bear witness to and kinship with the many millennia of Native American cooking traditions and the edible resources first exploited by Native Americans in Tuckaleechee Cove and the southern Appalachian Mountains.

Apparently the cove was situated along the border of two prehistoric culture areas, the South Appalachian and the Upper Tennessee Valley areas. To judge from differences in artifacts, particularly ceramic wares, each of these two culture areas enjoyed deep historical roots in the southern Appalachian Mountains on the one hand and the Tennessee Valley on the other. It is likely that the fortress walls (palisades) at Skittletown, discussed in chapter 2, signaled these cultural and perhaps sociopolitical differences between late prehistoric peoples of the cove and adjacent mountains.

The Big Dig, occasioned by the widening of US Highway 321 into the cove and along the Little River to the edge of the Great Smoky Mountains National Park, followed the path of an age-old transportation route, referred to as the "Great Indian Warpath," that traversed the Great Valley of the Tennessee River to the west with a major branch extending through Tuckaleechee Cove into and across the Great Smokies. William Myer's 1928 map (see figure 18) documented this and other traditional trails that connected Native Americans all across the extent of the southeastern United States. These trails probably date back to the very beginnings of human settlement in the Southeast towards the end of the Pleistocene. These ancient connections were the conduits for movement of materials such as new tool types, stone bowls, ceramic technology, and new ideas such as the iconography of the Middle Woodland Hopewell phenomenon.

Of course, archaeology rarely reveals much about belief systems other than iconography, or the physical symbols created as a part of the belief system. The archaeological research at the Big Dig produced little in the way of iconography. However, archaeologists do know a bit about the beliefs (religion and worldview) of southeastern Indians from early Euro-American accounts and Native American informants working with anthropologists in the early part of the twentieth century. The third section of chapter 2 briefly described the belief system of southeastern Indians (including the Cherokees), pointing out that their universe was inhabited by many beings other that humans.

Traditions of ghosts, spirits, supernatural beings, and haunts are not the exclusive province of Native American worldviews, but rather were brought to the New World by EuroAmerican immigrants and perhaps infused with notions from Native American forebears. A sense of fatalism and a sense of balance, maintained through proper living, also may have been inherited at least to some extent from the Native American antecedents in the southern Appalachian Mountains. Certainly a penchant for myths and storytelling are common bonds between ancient Native American and more recent residents of Tuckaleechee Cove and the Smoky Mountains.

Today, Tuckaleechee Cove is an area of motels, stables, hiking trails, and caverns that continue to entice people to visit well after the timber industry left the area. Marketing the area as a natural preserve on "the peaceful side of the Smokies," local residents wasted little time trying to entice people to stop and enjoy the area. Like farmers, millers, soldiers, and industrialists before them, travel writers have altered how people used and viewed Tuckaleechee Cove. Much of what they have written has reduced the area's history to what happened after the arrival of the Little River Lumber Company in 1901 and the establishment of the town of Townsend. The extensive prehistory and earlier historical origins of the rural community have been supplanted by the more convenient history of Townsend. These writers made Townsend, not the larger Tuckaleechee Cove, the predominant geographic and cultural center of the region, and in the process have changed how the community is represented in travel guides, maps, and the public's lexicon. As early as 1939, a Work Projects Administration (WPA) guidebook described Townsend as "a quiet village with many houses facing the river" with a hotel and tourist home. Tourism in Tuckaleechee Cove continued to develop as the popularity of the Great Smoky Mountains National Park grew. Small motels and restaurants catered to visitors who wanted to experience the Smokies. Maintaining its rural atmosphere, Tuckaleechee Cove stood in stark contrast to the over-commercialized glitz of Gatlinburg and Pigeon Forge, Tennessee, and Cherokee, North Carolina. Instead of tourist shops, go-cart tracks, and strip malls, the area focused heavily on a pseudo-form of ecotourism that relied heavily on manufactured cabins, horse trails, and hiking trails. Since the late 1930s the history and rural heritage of Tuckaleechee Cove have been lost among the more recent industrial and commercial history of Townsend.

The steady decline of Townsend stood out because it was a geographic and historical anomaly within the larger historical context of Tuckaleechee Cove. Townsend's economic and social development benefited the whole community but had little influence on those who chose to remain part of a more rural community with longer ties to tradition and heritage. Townsend did, of course, have a profound influence on Tuckaleechee Cove, and it is important to see that Tuckaleechee Cove's identity survived the loss of industry because it had been a well-rounded community before industry arrived. Nineteenth-century merchants, small producers, and farmers had created a local economy with wider ties to nearby towns and cities. Never isolated or economically backward, Tuckaleechee Cove thrived in the relative obscurity of the Great Smoky Mountains.

After 1939 nature reclaimed the landscape that had been temporarily altered by the timber industry. The region reminds the twenty-first century traveler of a rural past replete with sweeping mountain vistas and picturesque farms that dot Tuckaleechee Cove. *Tuckaleechee*, a Cherokee word assumed by English-speaking settlers, identified a region and community of people for hundreds of years.

As archaeologists and historians, the authors have attempted to tell the reader about the deep antiquity of Tuckaleechee Cove and the many faces that have looked out across the Little River and the cove's rolling plains. The stories dwelled on differences in cultures, technologies, and lifeways. While at first it may seem that the first people to see Tuckaleechee Cove were very different from those who live in and visit the cove today, there are connections—threads—that bind us with our past. So maybe the reader can agree that the many, many faces of Tuckaleechee Cove through the ages are in some ways not really so different after all.

Writing New Stories about the Past

Before the Big Dig in Tuckaleechee Cove, archaeologists knew very little about the artifacts and peoples who resided in the cove. Both archaeologists and historians were forced to base their reconstructions of lifeways and peoples on information from much better-known areas around or near the cove. The stories presented here will change in time. While archaeologists and historians cannot change the past, new information about the prehistoric and historic peoples of the cove will be discovered that will allow us to rewrite or add to the story of Tuckaleechee Cove.

INDEX